Employee Ambassadorship

Chris —
Best wishes,
Happy reading.

Michael Lowenstein

7/13/17

Employee Ambassadorship

Optimizing Customer-Centric Behavior from the Inside-Out and Outside-In

Michael W. Lowenstein

BUSINESS EXPERT PRESS

Employee Ambassadorship: Optimizing Customer-Centric Behavior from the Inside-Out and Outside-In

First published in 2017 by
Business Expert Press, LLC
222 East 46th Street, New York, NY 10017
www.businessexpertpress.com

ISBN-13: 978-1-63157-664-5 (paperback)
ISBN-13: 978-1-63157-665-2 (e-book)

Business Expert Press Marketing Strategy Collection

Collection ISSN: 2150-9654 (print)
Collection ISSN: 2150-9662 (electronic)

Cover and interior design by Exeter Premedia Services Private Ltd., Chennai, India

First edition: 2017

10 9 8 7 6 5 4 3 2 1

Printed in the United States of America.

Abstract

There have been a number of professional and academic studies, in multiple industries, linking employee attitudes and behaviors with the value customers perceive in their experiences. Through targeted research, and resultant training, communication, process, and reward and recognition programs, what we define as ambassadorship formalizes the direction in which employee engagement has been trending toward for years. Simply, the trend is optimizing employee commitment to the organization and its goals, to the company's unique value proposition, and to the customer. This is employee ambassadorship, a state beyond satisfaction and engagement where all employees are focused on, and tasked with, delivering customer value as part of their job description, irrespective of location, function or level.

Just as satisfaction has only incidental proven connection to customer experience and behavior, engagement has similar challenges for employees (and customers). Many companies are still measuring customer satisfaction in hopes that learning about its drivers will help build customer loyalty, but satisfaction isn't contemporary regarding decision making or reflective of what is going on in the customer's real, emotional world. The same can be said of engagement, applied to both customer and employee behavior.

"Employee engagement" has many meanings and interpretations, but relatively little of it has to do, by conceptual definition, specifically with impact on customer behavior and impact on the employee experience. Typically, there is little or no mention/inclusion of "customer" or "customer focus" elements in measurement or analysis, or in application such as training, of employee engagement. Though customer experience, and resultant behavior, is certainly impacted by engagement, it is more tangential and inferential than purposeful in nature.

There is growing general agreement that both developing employee ambassadors and customer advocates should receive high priority and emphasis if an enterprise is going to be successful. What building ambassadorship does mandate, however, is that having employees focus on the customer will definitely drive more positive experiences and stronger loyalty behavior (for both stakeholder groups). That is what the content/ scope of *Employee Ambassadorship* will help provide.

Keywords

advocacy, ambassadorship, behavior, communication, culture, customer experience, emotions, employee experience, empowerment, human resources, leadership, metrics, relationships, stakeholder, trust

Contents

Foreword

For Employees and Customers, Should the Goal Be Higher Engagement or Higher Experience Value?

Several years ago, in worldwide customer service experience research conducted for a major high-tech client, to drive stronger downstream customer behavior, it was found that support processes and agent–customer interaction had to take service employees well beyond the basics of knowledge, efficiency, and friendliness. Consistently, and irrespective of continent or country (over 60 countries, on 5 continents, were included in the study), the most effective reps showed true empathy for the customer's issue, literally "owning" or "wearing" the issue as if it were theirs as well, walking in their customer's shoes and making a true emotional connection.

What wasn't so completely understood at the time is that this level of employee commitment and personal investment also positively impacted the employee experience. This was something of an epiphany for our client, representing an unanticipated "bonus" result.

Customer experience (CX) pros can argue back and forth about whether a vendor can create deep emotions such as bonding and love in a customer. There are lots of articles and studies around stating things like "Highly engaged customers are loyal customers." There's little doubt that engaged customers can, and do, help shape the brand; and, engagement does influence customer behavior to some degree. They can also provide useful feedback and build brand-based communities. Today, is that enough?

From my perspective, at least, experiences that drive customers' emotional brand trust and bonding can be both shaped and sustained. That's

largely a function of organizational culture, customer-focused processes—
and the direct and indirect contribution of employees through ambassadorship behavior.

On the employee side of the equation, ambassadorship builds both
passion and partnership, enhancing the CX beyond engagement. And,
as importantly, it also enhances the employee experience, something
Human Capital Management (HCM) and HR execs are just coming to
realize and leverage.

There have been a number of professional and academic studies, in
multiple industries, linking employee attitudes and behaviors with the
value customers perceive in their experiences. Through targeted research,
and resultant training, communication, process, and reward and recognition programs, what we define as ambassadorship formalizes and extends
the direction in which employee engagement has been trending toward
for years. Simply, the trend is defined as optimizing and connecting
employee commitment to the organization and its goals, to the company's
unique value proposition, and to the customer. This creates a state where
all employees are focused on, and tasked with, delivering customer value
as part of their job description, irrespective of location, function, or level.

In other words, though there needs to be coordination and management of initiatives through HR and a CXO/CCO, everyone in the company, from the file clerk to the CEO, has this day-to-day responsibility
embedded within the job description.

This raises a classic chicken-and-egg question: Does focusing on the
employee, and the emotions inherent to creating and sustaining a positive
employee experience, generate as much benefit for the organization as
enhancing the CX or building employee engagement?

There is ongoing debate about which should be the priority. Several entire
books, in fact, have been written on this subject (such as *The Customer Comes
Second: Put Your People First and Watch 'em Kick Butt* by Hal Rosenbluth and
Diane Peters, and *Firms of Endearment: How World-Class Companies Profit
From Passion and Purpose* by Sheth, Sisodia, and Wolfe). There is general agreement that both developing employee ambassadors and customer advocates
should receive high parallel priority and emphasis if an enterprise is going to
be successful. What building ambassadorship does mandate, however, is that

having employees focus on the customer will definitely drive more positive experiences and stronger loyalty behavior for ***both*** stakeholder groups.

A recent article by a major employee research and engagement consulting organization reported on results of their national workforce tracking poll, the highlight of which was that employee engagement had risen 1.2 percent between January and February 2015 (to 32.9%) and that this new level was the highest engagement rate reported in the past three years.

The consulting organization went on to conclude from these findings that "recent trends suggest that improvements in engagement coincide with improvement in unemployment and underemployment," with the bottom-line statement that:

> A decline in the percentage of unemployed and underemployed Americans may have some influence on the percentage of engaged workers. As the job market for skilled employees becomes more competitive, it is possible that companies are putting more effort into engaging their current workers.

At best, this conclusion feels like a major s-t-r-e-t-c-h of correlation analysis results.

This same organization also stated that "employee engagement is a leading indicator of future business success"; and to the degree that engagement level can impact staff turnover and productivity, both identified as contributors to profitability, this can be accepted as a fair statement. However, when this organization, and others in the employee engagement research, training, and consultation space, make claims that engagement, in and of itself, contributes to customer value and loyalty behavior, two important questions need to be asked. Those questions are (1) Really? and (2) where's the consistent proof for individual companies?

Whenever encountering white papers that conflate the connection between employee engagement and happy customers, the earlier questions need to be asked. Further, there is no specific connection to the emotional drivers of employee experience or, for that matter, to CX. Emotions, understood on an accepted negative-to-positive hierarchy (see Figure F.1), are critical to understanding experience and behavior.

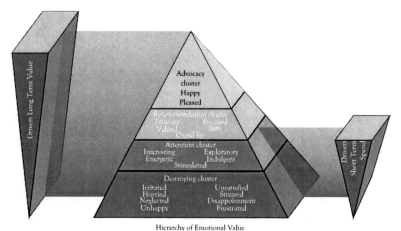

Hierarchy of Emotional Value

Figure F.1 Hierarchy of emotional value

Source: Beyond Philosophy (www.beyondphilosophy.com).

Just as satisfaction has little proven connection to customer behavior, employee engagement was neither specifically designed to drive customer behavior nor was it designed to enhance the employee's experience. To build on this statement, let's begin by looking at the results of satisfaction on downstream customer action. Beyond extremely macroconnection to sales, customer satisfaction (as expressed through the American Customer Satisfaction Index [ACSI]) has been shown to have little direct connection to purchase behavior, to the tune of 0.0 to 0.1 percent correlation. Many companies are still measuring customer satisfaction in hopes that learning about its drivers will help build customer loyalty behavior, but satisfaction isn't contemporary regarding longitudinal experience and decision making, or reflective of what is going on in the customer's real, emotional world.

As discussed on multiple occasions, and as proven in our own research, "employee engagement" has many meanings and interpretations, but relatively little of it has to do, at least by conceptual definition, specifically with impact on customer behavior. Typically, there is little or no mention/inclusion of "customer" or "customer focus" elements in either measurement or analysis of employee engagement.

Though there is proof that CX, and resultant behavior, is somewhat impacted by engagement, it is more tangential and inferential than purposeful in nature. Further, according to Gallup, the "needle" pointing to changes in national and global levels of employee engagement has not moved in the past 10 to 15 years, making it an ongoing challenge to connect employee experience to CX.

A 2015 *Advertising Age* blog by a leading marketing research consulting organization encapsulated employee ambassadorship very well: Ambassadorship should be an enterprisewide mantra for every organization:

> All employees need to embody the intended customer experience. A narrative must be cascaded down to every single individual in the organization. Your employees must clearly understand their role in delivering the promise the narrative makes to the end customer. This requires multiple conversations and socialization across all business divisions and at every level, not just for customer support roles.

To that quote, I say Amen.

In my 2011 book *The Customer Advocate and The Customer Saboteur: Linking Social Word-of-Mouth, Brand Impression, and Stakeholder Behavior*, here is how this was encapsulated:

> You cannot create, or sustain, customer loyalty behavior without committed employees. The key is to focus on developing and supporting employees so that they, in turn, focus on the customer and the customer experience. Ideally, you want every employee to be an ambassador. Employee ambassadorship is a framework for linking employee commitment to business results by emphasizing the need for the entire organization to create unique, value-add customer experiences. Optimizing customer experience is everybody's job.

One of the key objectives of this book is to compare and contrast the enterprise and stakeholder benefits of employee experience and ambassadorship relative to HR-focused engagement, or other more antecedent ways of thinking about their contribution and commitment. Let's begin.

Introduction

Do You Really Wanna Work Here? Are You Happy? Are You Aligned? Are You Productive?

Oh, By the Way, Do You Understand How You Contribute to Optimizing Customer Experiences?

And … as an employee, are you:

a. Loyal to the organization?
b. Committed to the success, goals, values, and objectives of the enterprise?
c. Proud to work for the organization?
d. Positive about the organization?
e. Aware, in current terms, of how customers perceive the experience and value they receive from the organization?

Can you also say how likely you'll be to still be employed there in the next year?

Great! Terrific! Or, as my British pals might say, tickety-boo or brilliant! According to many HR consulting and training organizations, that makes you aligned and engaged (though not necessarily productive). Maybe you're also satisfied, even happy, both of which are short term and tactical states of mind for an employee. Is that enough to create ambassadorship, where helping optimize customer experiences (CXs) is (or should be) in everyone's job description?

Employee ambassadorship, connected to but distinctive from employee satisfaction and employee engagement, is defined (like engagement) as commitment to the organization itself and the value represented by its products and services, but it goes further. Ambassadorship is also, uniquely, commitment to customers.

In identifying levels ambassadorship within an organization, we also ask employees the following questions:

a. How often do you tell others how good the company's products and services are?

b. How often do you tell others how bad the company's products and services are?

c. How often do you tell others how good the company is as a place to be employed?

d. How often do you tell others how bad the company is as a place to be employed?

e. How strongly would you recommend the company as a place to work?

f. Do the company's products and services exceed customer expectations, even delight them?

Ambassadorship, supportive of customer centricity initiatives, especially as they impact experiences and relationships, directly links employee behavior to these outcomes. In addition, it enhances the employee experience. To understand how we have arrived at ambassadorship, and the value it represents for organizations, we can begin with the ServQual Model. The ServQual Model is now over 30 years old. And, while some of it remains very useful and applicable—particularly striving for value delivery perceptual alignment between employees and customers—we are living in a vastly different world today, for both employees and customers.

It's understood that stakeholder decision dynamics are far more emotional and relationship based than was considered in 1985, when ServQual was created by three progressive marketing academics (Berry, Parasuraman, Zeithaml, *Delivering Quality Service: Balancing Customer Perceptions and Expectations*). As noted, employee satisfaction elements are largely tactical and rational in nature; and to influence key elements of CX, even employee engagement, as defined, has only inferential and superficial effect.

While I'm taking on established models, I'll also include the venerable and venerated Service-Profit Chain, which is addressed in more detail later in the book. Unfortunately, the Service-Profit Chain, important as a means of linking customers and employees when it first appeared, misses some key contemporary realities. As stated in one of my blogs on the subject from a few years ago:

> The Service-Profit chain postulated that employee satisfaction drives customer satisfaction.
>
> Today's demanding and continuously changing customer environment requires actionable tools for better understanding of both customer behavioral drivers and drivers of employee attitude and action that extend well beyond conventional-wisdom communication and satisfaction feedback approaches.

The full blog has been viewed almost 3,000 times, so it seems to have struck a chord.

Ambassadorship recognizes that there's a definite, and powerful, linkage of stakeholder groups and their behavior. Customers who actively (vocal, level of favorability, reduced consideration set, etc.) express their personal commitment to a supplier, based on individual experience and memory, can be strongly positive (advocates and brand loyalists), neutral, or negative (saboteurs). The level of commitment and advocacy/bonding is based on customers' rational and emotional response to experiences and relationships.

Employees, similarly, can significantly impact CX and resultant loyalty behavior toward their employer through a range of attitudes and behaviors on behalf of the brand, company, and customer. These attitudes and behaviors, like those of customers, can range from highly positive, to indifferent, to highly negative Figure I.1.

Great companies—Google, Southwest Airlines, Wegmans, Amazon, Zappos, Whole Foods Market, and Trader Joe's—with great, progressive leaders understand alignment and integration between these stakeholder groups. They are fully aware of what practicing ambassadorship and optimized stakeholder experience, within the culture and across the

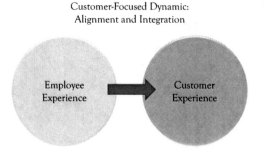

Customer-Focused Dynamic:
Alignment and Integration

Figure I.1 Relationship of employee experience to customer experience

Source: Beyond Philosophy (www.beyondphilosophy.com).

entire enterprise, can mean for the organization, its customers, and its employees. The perspectives of these exemplars on the value of human capital as an internal brand-building mechanism, is one of the key factors in what makes them great, and they are fully explored in *Employee Ambassadorship*.

CHAPTER 1

The Evolving Role(s) and Needs of Employees ... and How to Stay in Front of Them

Apart from customer loyalty, which is on the radar screen of just about every company, there is no other topic that concerns organizations more than employee retention, commitment, and productivity. Staff turnover is near 20-year highs for many companies. Two research firms, Walker Information and Hudson Institute, recently joined forces to conduct a nationwide employee loyalty study. Their results confirmed that staff loyalty and commitment are in short supply:

- Only 24 percent of employees consider themselves truly loyal, committed to their organization and its goals, and planning to stay at least two years.
- Thirty-three percent of employees were high risk, not committed, and not planning to stay.
- Thirty-nine percent were classified as trapped. They plan to stay, but are not committed to their organization.
- Among those who felt they worked for an ethical organization, 55 percent were truly loyal. For those who didn't feel they worked for an ethical organization, the loyalty figure was 9 percent.

The 72 percent of employees identified as being at risk or trapped represent another key, yet less explored, concern for companies. The lack of employee commitment frequently translates to having poor personal experiences, and being out of alignment, with each other and with customers, in executing the company's mission, goals, and strategic objectives and in appropriately representing the product or service value proposition. In other words, what they are doing on the job can be counterproductive and damaging, to themselves and others. Since the issues impacting customer loyalty and commitment to a supplier are often highly correlated with staff productivity and proaction, optimizing employee loyalty and commitment becomes doubly important.

Many companies don't even realize the depth of their staff retention, continuity, and alignment problems. While at the senior management level, turnover may only be 4 to 5 percent, the real drain of talent is typically among those employees who are age 25 to 35 years and have been at the same firm for 3 to 10 years.

These staff members are often among the most productive and represent the highest long-term contribution potential for any company. They can also be among the most nonaligned with company vision and strategy, and noninvested in their commitment to customers. Yet, the vast majority of organizations don't track the drivers of turnover, threats of defection, or misalignment among this important group.

This "silent" defection and misalignment is particularly prevalent in large, decentralized companies with 20 to 100 divisions, operating in multiple states and/or multiple continents. On a single division basis, the defection and misalignment numbers among staff age 25 to 35 years may not seem problematic. But when viewed across all divisions of a company, the churn, potential defection, and misalignment numbers in this age group are often alarmingly high.

Firms pay a big price for staff defection, or "shadow" defection, where personal performance and commitment levels are very low. For starters, when employees leave a company, it has often been found that customers are soon to follow. Recent customer defection studies have shown that roughly 70 percent of the reasons customers churn can be traced back to issues related to staff's lack of commitment and turnover. And staff turnover often leads to more, and more widespread, staff turnover, spreading like an epidemic (see Figure 1.1). Even the departure of a single valuable employee can send "shock waves" through a company culture, leaving remaining staff demoralized and disillusioned. If there was a trend toward

Figure 1.1 Defection note

Source: Internet.

misalignment, high staff turnover, and/or low morale and disaffection, will only cause it to increase.

Replacing the departed employee is expensive. Human resource executives estimate that when all direct and indirect factors are considered—the recruitment fees, discontinuity from defector's lost leads and contacts, the new employee's reduced productivity while learning the new job, and the time and energy co-workers spend guiding the newbie—replacement costs are estimated at approximately 150 percent, or more, of the departing person's salary.

Misalignment, too, carries a high price tag, though it's more challenging to isolate and estimate than the direct loss of an employee. A lack of alignment can be seen in places like the organization's style and culture, staff communication, teamwork, and information flow, service to/focus on customers, level of training offered, productivity and efficiency, and management effectiveness.

Responsibilities and Opportunities in Customer Service: Behavioral Alignment Example

Research studies in multiple industries indicate that customer service representatives (CSRs) across the United States handle an average of 2,000 customer interactions each week. If CSRs are not aligned with the customer strategy, indeed are not directly involved with creating and executing the strategy as part of their own job experience, this can represent 2,000 opportunities to put customers at risk or lose them.

Placing the customer first, or completely focusing on customers—two of the clarion calls of customer centricity—have a hollow ring if these strategies aren't drilled down and reduced to a point where CSRs' daily efforts can have a positive impact on customer loyalty behavior. The reality is, however, that few organizations do this. Instead, they set unrealistic customer service productivity requirements or establish performance metrics and levels that are not based on customer input or need. Further, because customer service centers (aka customer contact centers, call centers, or interaction centers) haven't, until recently, begun to be seen as profit generation centers, their vision and mission, as well as their operational construct, was seen in fairly myopic terms.

These centers of customer contact now represent the principal touch point with customers; and, beyond technology, the centers have the capability to generate and manage a continuous flow of customer information and to increase customer loyalty. Getting the most out of customer contact centers, indeed from employees in all customer-facing and non-customer-facing functions, will require change; and, in many companies, this means significant change.

For commitment and what we describe as ambassadorship to be optimized, one of the changes that companies will have to institute will be to start focusing on people. Tremendous investments have been made on technological innovations—interactive voice response (IVR) systems, call routing, multimedia integration, and the like—yet investment in people, and processes to support them, has been stagnant, lagging behind other efforts. To deliver on the promise technology offers in customer relationships, staff performance and experience have to be prioritized. People have to be shown what to do, given feedback about how they're doing, and rewarded if they are doing well.

Meeting the objectives of a customer relationship management (CRM) or customer experience (CX) strategy means, for one thing, that targets and metrics set for CSRs must be balanced to incorporate productivity, quality of service delivered, and effectiveness of performance on behalf of customers. One of the most effective ways for accomplishing this, we have found, is through "customer-first" teams, in customer service and throughout the company.

Tom Peters has said that, in the future, "most work will be done by project teams. The 'average' team will consist of various people from various 'organizations' with various skills. Networks of bits and pieces of companies will come together to exploit a market opportunity." Such can certainly be the case with customer loyalty, customer service, and customer recovery programs.

There are several advantages to networked, team-based structures as opposed to traditional hierarchies as they strive to create value and higher trust levels for customers. They include better, more quickly shared information, greater decision agility, faster response time, and greater, more proactive, and relationship-building customer contact, as well as:

- Flattened, matrix-based organizational structures for greater efficiency
- Minimizing nonvalue-added functional activities and better use of staff time and talent
- Assigning ownership of performance
- Greater opportunity for self-management and a wider scope of work in each job, with more (rotated) exposure to customers
- Linking performance objectives and individual and team performance to customer loyalty behavior
- More targeted employee training and skill development

A fitting example of how customer-first teams can impact customer loyalty and customer winback—and staff loyalty and performance as well—comes from Baptist Health Care in Pensacola, Florida. Several years ago, Baptist Health Care had patient service performance, which ranked them close to the bottom of all hospitals in national surveys. This situation also contributed to both declining patient populations and low staff morale.

Baptist Health Care executives were determined to turn this around. Quint Studer, then the hospital's president, said, "We had to create the type of environment where people drive by two other hospitals to get here." Baptist Health Care formed 10 cross functional employee teams to examine every aspect of value delivery to patients and their families. More than 150 hospital employees now participate as team members on these original teams. Each team has membership as diverse as corporate vice presidents and cafeteria workers. Additionally, Baptist has created ad hoc and ongoing teams to address areas such as customer winback. Up to 30 percent of Baptist Health Care employees serve on teams at any given time.

Today, Baptist Health Care's service performance ranks among the very best in national customer surveys, its market share has significantly improved, staff morale is higher, and staff loss—and the money previously spent for recruiting as a result of turnover—has dramatically declined.

Baptist Health Care is now using their superior performance in patient care and services as a springboard for moving to an even higher plateau. As described by Pam Bilbrey, formerly Baptist Health Care's senior vice president of Development: "We're pushing ourselves to move past the passion of service excellence to the next stage: customer loyalty." A testament to the success of Baptist Health Care is the organization's consistent naming to a high position on *Fortune* magazine's annual list of the 100 best companies to work for in America.

The array of cross functional customer-first team possibilities is limited only by an organization's willingness to embrace the concept. Bottom line: Customer-first teams enhance loyalty and staff productivity. Baptist Health Care is an excellent example of the success of customer-first teams. Every company should want to emulate their achievements. We have more to say about Baptist Health Care in Chapter 5.

Companies are also going to have to do a better job of determining just how effective service groups are at creating perceived customer value and, ultimately, optimizing customer loyalty behavior.

Traditional employee satisfaction studies, just like customer satisfaction studies, are much more about measuring superficial attitudes and past events, keying largely on salaries and benefits, and the working environment, than they are about understanding emotional components of the job experience, how aligned staff are with customers and with fellow employees in delivering consistently superior experiences, how productive staff are on behalf of customers, and how well supported and directed they are in providing value.

For customer-facing groups like customer service to have the same type of contribution, alignment with goals, and leadership seen in organizations like Baptist Health Care, and for these groups to help realize the promise of customer centricity, the three words that need to be emphasized are *training, involvement,* and *measurement.*

A Quick "How-to" Primer for Getting to Staff Loyalty, Alignment, and Commitment Optimization

Having reviewed hundreds of traditional employee satisfaction and engagement surveys over the years, and carefully studying how the results have been interpreted and applied by companies, it's clear that the vast majority of them are about as superficial and challenged to provide real direction to corporate and HR management as their customer satisfaction survey cousins.

Employee commitment study results are, as noted, often mirror images of what's going on with customers. For example, one of our clients was known to have a highly ineffectual regional director. In that director's region, both customer and staff defection were quite high. On the staff loyalty and alignment study for the client, regional employees rated teamwork and staff communication dramatically lower than for other regions, especially among frontline staff. Likewise, the customer loyalty scores for that same region were also low, with particularly poor performance on customer communication and responsiveness. Bottom line, staff loyalty, focus, and alignment problems ultimately become customer problems. There was little commitment evidenced by employees. Thus, the linkage between stakeholder group perception and behavior was pretty easy to both isolate and correct.

Compared to traditional employee satisfaction and engagement research, there's a lot to know about identifying the drivers of ambassadorial behavior. Here are some quick guidelines to keep you on track.

Avoid Measuring Employee Satisfaction

Satisfaction has a strong tendency to deal with attitudes and not behaviors. Also, satisfaction has proven to be poorly correlated with actual loyalty and productive behavior. For example, a recent employee study showed that only 10 percent said they were dissatisfied with their employers and their jobs, but 25 percent said they would search for a new job within a year. Instead, ask questions that measure your company's performance as an employer (i.e., "On a scale from 1 to 5, rate our performance as your employer") and other question areas that we recommend.

Measure Employees' Likelihood to Remain with You and Contribute to Your Success

Likewise, measure your employees' likelihood to recommend the company, or otherwise communicate in positive ways, to other potential employees (i.e., "On a scale from 1 to 5, how likely are you to recommend the company to other potential employees?"). Also, recognize and reward employees for length of service to the enterprise (Figure 1.2).

Develop Specific Job Statements

Detailed elements of day-to-day activity must first be generated (often through qualitative research)—about key aspects of their working life, relationships, how they are guided and supported, and so on, to be presented to all employees for performance and importance evaluation. These are known as attributes. I recommend that attributes be customized, rather than be identical to those applied at other companies, because the culture and operating processes of each company are unique. In your staff ambassadorship and commitment study, you will want to include attribute statements that address each of the following six themes:

Figure 1.2 Employee loyalty award

Source: Internet.

- *Cohesion*—These attributes address teamwork and communication between and within groups, plus work quality, effectiveness, and staff/management interaction.
- *Morale/culture*—These attributes address the "fabric" of the organization, consideration of staff needs, and place of employment.
- *Career security/growth*—These attributes address the employees' sense of "shared destiny," or belief that the company will support their security, growth, and career development.
- *Business confluence*—These attributes address the extent to which employees partner and participate in the company's vision, mission, and strategic objectives.
- *Customer focus*—These attributes address the employees' opinions of the company's proaction and responsiveness with customers and how the tools they are provided help with that goal.
- *Management effectiveness*—These attributes address employees' views of how well people and processes are managed.

Ask Staff Members to Rank Elements of Their Jobs

And ask to explain their reasons for those rankings. Employees should also be asked to state reasons for low attribute and overall performance ratings, providing quantified anecdotal depth to the ratings data.

Identify Areas of Expressed and Unexpressed Staff Complaints

When unexpressed, determine the reasons. When expressed, ask about outcomes. Look at (model) the impact of complaints, especially those frequently stated, on staff loyalty.

Model the Impact of Attribute Performance and Importance on Staff Loyalty and Commitment to Customers

Report key findings and modeled results. Within the report, draw conclusions and make recommendations. Take action, including reporting findings back to staff.

Ask staff for their feedback because it implies a commitment by management for action based on findings. Report findings in a timely manner to staff along with an action plan for addressing key concerns. Do this and you'll help grow employee trust and strengthen loyalty and alignment. Don't do it, and employees will likely blow off your next staff survey. Our quantitative methods are built around self-completion interviews, and they include online staff loyalty data collection, which enables almost real-time analysis and reporting of findings, conclusions, and recommendations to staff and management.

Some Key Takeaway Thoughts

Higher levels of training, more involvement in strategy development and execution, and appropriate staff performance and alignment measurement will, increasingly, differentiate companies that are merely good from those that are great. For customer service, because they are so close to customers and so involved with creating and sustaining loyalty behavior, the stakes are particularly high. Whether inside or outsourced, customer service must be completely aligned with, and supportive of, corporate customer loyalty goals and initiatives.

In our 2001 book, *Customer WinBack: How to Recapture Lost Customers—And Keep Them Loyal*, coauthor Jill Griffin and I identified nine "best practices" for building staff commitment and ambassadorship. The following is distilled and summarized from about 20 pages in the book.

Build a Climate of Trust and Authenticity That Works Both Ways

Employees appreciate and respond to empowerment and opportunities to learn and contribute. For most employees, trust is shown in one important way when they can manage their own time and resources. Trust needs to be woven into the company's mission and vision statement, and there should be a certain amount of transparency, and a free flow of information, between management and staff. This will also help mitigate negative communication and gossip. Per a recent Edelman Trust Barometer study, nearly one in three employees don't trust their employer, so it has become an increasing challenge to generate positive vocal support and behavior.

Trust is particularly important, an emotional underpinning of employee behavior. Considered in classic psychological terms, trust is viewed as somewhat more a "feeder," or building block, of emotion. We typically see emotions (as defined by experts like Paul LeDoux, Silvan Tomkins, Paul Ekman, and Robert Plutchik) as including surprise, interest, joy, rage, fear, disgust, shame, and anguish, and also happiness and sadness, or acceptance and anticipation. As regards both b2b and b2c relationships between customers and suppliers, lack of confidence is driven by insecurity and egotism, and the ability to be confident is based on feelings of safety and acceptance. The name of the emotion-based game, with confidence as a ground rule, is "trustworthiness."

Stakeholder behavior research studies consistently show that elements of vendor or employer trust, represented by image, reputation, and expressions of positive values such as sincerity and honesty, are significant drivers of loyalty and disloyalty, advocacy and alienation, and bonding and rejection. Trust is an essential building block of the Maslow values hierarchy.

Emotions and their leveraging impact are given an entire chapter of treatment later in the book; however, it is essential to label their contribution to behavior early on.

Train, Train, Train and Cross-Train

Task-related, and nontask-related, training is seen by many employees as the company's faith and investment in them. Training is the most productive and effective form of employee recognition and development; however, it is often the most vulnerable to budget cutbacks. Cross-training helps foster cohesiveness, involvement, and leadership; and training should be considered beyond the employee's immediate functional area to create more well-rounded, knowledgeable, and contributory employees. Note: Over 80 percent of Southwest Airlines employees are cross-trained in at least one other function every year as one method of building leadership.

Make Sure Each Employee Has a Defined Career Path

Provide tools so employees can inventory talents and elements of experience, and encourage movement within the company. Many leading-edge companies find they can build leadership and loyalty by enabling employees to move freely into different groups.

Provide Frequent Evaluations and Reviews

Effective feedback systems play a big role in keeping employees productive and committed to their jobs and to the company. Research studies consistently find employees are emphatic in their desire for as much feedback from management and peers as they can get. Don't wait to do this on an annual or semiannual basis. Do it as frequently as possible ("just-in-time," if this is workable) as it will help the employee grow and develop. Also, bottom-up feedback, where employees provide insight as to what management can do to make them more effective and productive, should be built into the review model.

Seek to Inform, Seek to Debrief

Employees often complain that, even though they are working harder than ever, their thoughts about anything beyond their immediate jobs are rarely sought. Schedule frequent update meetings featuring employee input and contributions. Some companies have "radical inclusion" approaches: Arranging for people to hear news at exactly the same time sends a signal that everyone is valued and everyone is "in the know." Other organizations have novel ways of communicating with staff—from panel discussions to town meetings—they use a variety of forums to connect with staff.

Recognize and Reward Initiative

Best-in-class companies don't just do the expected for customers. They create top-end experiences, in part through proactive and committed employees. One of the key ways this happens is by fostering a culture that recognizes and rewards initiative. Employees should be both recognized and rewarded for building customer value (i.e., relationship building, creative solutions, empowered achievements, cross functional involvement). When designing such programs, it should be kept in mind that these initiatives are rarely expensive, so the "we can't afford it" trap should be avoided. Also, companies should make clear distinctions between recognition and reward. The recognition should be special, a real token of appreciation that singles out the employee for his or her contribution. As noted earlier in the chapter, especially for cohesive, stakeholder-centric cultural purposes, it is also important to recognize and reward length of service to the organization.

Ask Employees What They Want (and Give It to Them)

Conduct ambassadorship, linkage, and alignment research to find out how productive and loyal employees are and how well they are supported and guided in building value and equity for customers. Avoid measuring employee satisfaction because, like customer satisfaction, traditional employee studies provide relatively little useful direction. Also, survey results (and plans being developed as a product of survey findings) should be shared with staff in an expeditious manner.

By All Means, Have Fun!

Use creative means to give a lighter, more family-oriented "feel" to company culture. Ideas can include events around holidays, having an open house for family members, special recognition prizes, and so on. Some companies, recognizing that "playing together means staying together," have initiated novel approaches to lighten daily grinds. Ben & Jerry's, for instance, has a "Grand Poobah of Joy" who gives entertaining messages over the office intercom, accompanied by harmonica music (and employees also get two free pints of ice cream per day). Recognizing that happy employees do not necessarily equal happy customers, they also blend in more practical approaches for culture building.

Hire the Right Employees in the First Place

Profile top performers to identify success factors, and make recruiting top talent a key corporate value. Some companies, such as Southwest Airlines, even make customers part of the employee recruiting process. Other organizations keep detailed records on their recruiting efforts, including debriefing both successful and unsuccessful candidates.

Creating a culture within the organization that nurtures loyalty, commitment, and productivity from the moment the new hire walks through the door and throughout the life cycle of the employee will go a long way to sustaining customer loyalty. The good news is that employees, particularly those in customer service, will want to be active contributors to that effort. As *Fortune* magazine columnist Thomas Stewart has said, "Human beings want to pledge allegiance to something. The desire to belong is a foundation value, underlying all others." When that "something" is the optimization of customer loyalty behavior, to repeat the guiding conclusion of Hal Rosenbluth, everybody wins.

Why Should All Employees Be Focused on, and Tasked with, Delivering Customer Value?

The quick answer is because it's the smartest, and most customer-centric, productive, and profitable thing for any enterprise to practice. Here are some definitive reasons:

- *First reason*: The powerful link that exists between employee attitudes/behaviors vis-a-vis customers and CX.

  There have been a number of professional and academic studies, in multiple industries, linking employee attitudes and behaviors with the value customers perceive in their experiences. Through targeted research, and resultant training, communication, process, and reward and recognition programs, what we define as ambassadorship formalizes the direction in which employee engagement has been trending toward for years. Simply, the trend is optimizing employee commitment to the organization and its goals, to the company's unique value proposition, and to the customer. This is employee ambassadorship, a state where all employees are focused on, and tasked with, delivering customer value as part of their job description, irrespective of location, function, or level (see Figure 1.3).

Figure 1.3 Employee interacting with customer

Source: Internet.

In other words, though there needs to be coordination and management of initiatives through HR and a CXO/CCO, everyone in the company, from the file clerk to the CEO, has this day-to-day responsibility embedded within the job description. So, while the ambassadorship research framework, which we use to identify the degree of linkage between employee attitudes/behavior and customer behavior, does include questions on job satisfaction and belief in the organization, the core is really about specific employee behavior and a set of beliefs based on experience as a staff member.

- *Second reason*: Focusing on deep and vocal commitment, which we define as ambassadorship, creates the same positive financial and employee behavior results as focusing on CX.

This is a classic chicken-and-egg question, that is, whether focusing on the employee generates as much benefit for the organization as enhancing CX; and there is ongoing debate about which should be the priority. Several entire books, in fact, have been written on this subject (such as *The Customer Comes Second: Put Your People First and Watch 'em Kick Butt* by Hal Rosenbluth and Diane Peters, and *Firms of Endearment: How World-Class Companies Profit From Passion and Purpose* by Sheth, Sisodia, and Wolfe). There is general agreement that both developing employee ambassadors and customer advocates should receive high priority and emphasis if an enterprise is going to be successful. What building ambassadorship does mandate, however, is that having employees focus on the customer will definitely drive more positive experiences and stronger loyalty behavior.

- *Third reason*: As noted earlier, employee engagement is principally about productivity, degree of "fit," and alignment, and tells an organization little about level or degree of customer centricity.

Our employee ambassadorship research, about which there is more to say later in the book, includes multiple categories of attributes, many of which would be found, in one form or another, in engagement studies: cohesion, satisfaction, business alignment, career and growth, management effectiveness, and morale and culture. What employee engagement studies don't include, however, is customer focus as a key attribute category, with diagnostics such as:

- o The functions I perform contribute to the company's delivery of customer value.
- o Cross-training enables me to provide better value to customers.
- o The company is customer focused.
- o I understand customers' value priorities.
- o Management listens to my ideas on creating value for customers.
- o The company has a clearly defined mission for creating customer value.
- o New products and services for customers are clearly communicated within the company.
- o I have the tools and resources I need to provide value to customers.

This is just a small sample. In our research, we typically include between 20 and 25 customer focus attributes. What they reveal speaks volumes about the degree of cross enterprise customer centricity by various groups within a company. Bottom line: Employee engagement may claim to influence customer behavior, and this is true in the way customer satisfaction influences customer behavior. In other words, it is incidental, passive, and superficial. Ambassadorship, purposely, chooses a different path, the path of employee focus on customers, à la Robert Frost's classic poem, *The Road Not Taken*:

Two roads diverged in a wood, and I—
I took the one less traveled by,
And that has made all the difference.

Pushing Past Employee Satisfaction and Engagement

Just as with customers, it's essential to the delivery of value that optimizing experience for employees—well beyond satisfaction and engagement—is an organizational priority. We talk a lot about how customer value has two components: a rational, functional side and an emotional, relationship side. Most companies focus on optimizing the functional side of customer value, through quality management and process improvement.

While things like that can be important when it comes to meeting customers' basic expectations, they often aren't particularly differentiating; and they don't drive long-term customer trust and loyalty. Trust and loyalty are more frequently engendered by the emotional connection with the company. And, this is where behavior of customers is fostered by attitudes and actions of employees, toward the customers, supported by the experiences employees have on the job.

More than satisfaction and engagement, more than commitment to the company or the brand, more than commitment to productivity or innovation or even the organization itself, what we are talking about is enterprise-level commitment to optimizing the stakeholder experience.

Customer market research provides the data and the insights about behavior drivers. The biggest impact this has rests in demonstrating the difference between internal perception of value and external perception.

This, as we'll demonstrate later in the book, can also be applied to employee research. For example, service managers and representatives, salespeople, and other employees are often out of sync with customers in terms of perceived value of services, products, and features.

One way to uncover just how out of sync employees are with customers is to "mirror" customer surveys. For example, ask representatives from the organization to answer questions posed to customers as they believe the customers themselves would answer them. Conducting this kind of research will quickly uncover the gaps in perception and help highlight the need for change. This is closely related to one of the key perceptual gaps identified in the ServQual Model, that is, between employees and customers.

For their part, HR can help institutionalize and formalize narrowing this perceptual gap; they can help cascade this out to the rest of the organization. You want and need their help, but you also need to make sure that you are building in redundancies and diagnostics so that they feel comfortable. More important, senior management needs to get everyone marching behind the banner of optimizing the customer and employee experience. They need to state and restate this again and again. Before they do that, of course, they have to accept that organizational focus is the problem. And that can be a real challenge.

Here's a personal story to illustrate what I mean. I've sat with managers and executives during focus groups with customers talking about the value received and relationships with specific vendors, and when these managers and executives hear what the customers are saying about them, their employees, and their business, I've seen armed insurrection break out behind the glass. The managers and executives refuse to believe what they are hearing, but the fact that they don't get what the customer gets is the real lesson. They are in denial, and they are usually very much mistaken. They don't get that what matters to the customer is the emotional, relationship side of the value equation.

So, a key and fundamental question needs to be asked, "Who in the organization doesn't own the relationship with the customer, either directly or indirectly?" Recalling the work of W. Edwards Deming, he believed that everyone in the organization is "either serving the customer or supporting someone who does." This means that the ideal of employee and CX needs to permeate the entire company.

Unfortunately, this is rarely the case. Instead, many companies find that about 10 percent of their staff exhibit strong commitment and other performance qualities, 15 percent may be actively sabotaging the customer relationship, and the remaining 75 percent are neither saboteurs nor committed. Organizations need to do some analysis to find out where there is overlap between the behaviorally elite and the rank and file. What is dragging them down, and what are they already doing that just needs to be encouraged?

At one client, we determined that about 10 to 15 percent of their staff fell into the saboteur category. They asked, "Should we fire them?" Our answer was, "No." They had a systemic problem in terms of organizational focus that needed to be addressed. Unless you change what you care about, what you emphasize, the problem will just repeat itself.

The real issue is this: Do you want everyone to have both great experiences and be committed, and are you willing to do what it takes to get them there? Employees, as agents, need to bring passion, emotion, and empowerment to their own experiences and to the CX. They need to be value driven, not process driven; and they need to be supported in doing this. That's the focus of everything being covered in *Employee Ambassadorship*.

CHAPTER 2

Customer Centricity and Stakeholder Centricity, and the "People-First" Employee Experience

Customer Centricity Versus Customer Friendliness Versus Product Centricity

My colleague Peter Fader is the codirector of Wharton School's Customer Analytics Initiative, and author of *Customer Centricity: What It Is, What It Isn't, and Why It Matters* (Wharton Digital Press, Philadelphia, 2011), so he understands the section title topics quite well. In the podcast produced to help promote the book, Professor Fader explained the differences between customer centricity and customer friendliness. In customer-friendly companies, all customers are served in an equally positive way.

While on the surface, customer friendliness appears to be a desirable concept and objective, it is frequently suboptimal because at these friendly companies, there is, for all intents and purposes, no actionable customer segmentation, and certainly no microsegmentation or individualized, personalized focus on the experience. The reality is that all customers are NOT created equal, and never will be, even with the most targeted and sophisticated of prospecting approaches; but customer-friendly companies usually don't recognize that fact. Poor customers are served as well as excellent customers, so this is an inefficient use of resources. In such companies, there is little lifetime value data (purchase and downstream advocacy behavior) generated, or leveraged, for segments or individual customers.

Next, many companies are actively product centric. As stated by Professor Fader, they believe that strategic advantage is based on elements inherent in the product or service and the expertise behind that product or service.

In product-centric companies, the organizational structure (divisions, groups, and teams) are typically set up around products, employees are rewarded based on their ability to sell existing products or create new products, and brand or corporate equity is seen as having greater value than the customer. There are, however, cracks in this concept, due principally to the realities of globalization, speed of new technologies, deregulation, and the rising power of consumers (to get what they want, when they want it, and from whomever they select to provide it).

Some companies, principally FMCGs like Coca-Cola and P & G, will (and should, according to Professor Fader) continue to be largely brand focused and product centric because of the difficulty of getting data on an individual customer basis. For the rest, product centricity puts them at risk relative to companies that are customer centric.

Customer centricity, as Professor Fader pointed out, is a strategy to fundamentally align a company's products and services with the wants and needs of its best customers and those which can readily be bootstrapped (through research segmentation tools such as advocacy behavior level) to become more financially attractive. It is about identifying the most valuable customers and then doing everything possible to bring their (positive and negative) ideas into the center of the enterprise, create value for them, generate revenue from them, and to find more customers like them.

That strategy has a specific business outcome goal: more profits for the long term. This objective is one that every enterprise would like to achieve; and, it can be attained if an organization is willing to move past outdated ideas about customer–company relations and rethink organizational design, key performance metrics, product development, and resource allocation. It also requires, I'd suggest, different thinking about the role and contribution of employees.

Notes on Successfully Moving to Customer Centricity (from Customers Inside, Customers Outside)

Building and sustaining a customer-centric culture is core to successful enterprise performance. However, once the basic architectural and engineering components are functional—or, in concert with their functionality—organizations must make certain that their strategy and tactics for optimizing customer experience (CX), and downstream behavior, are both contemporary and effective. This includes elements of branding, messaging, and communication, and maintaining strong, proactive value-based relationships, as well as optimizing employee behavior (Figure 2.1).

For companies seeking to build trust and optimize CX delivery, they need not only a customer-centric culture, but also the strategy and tactics for building an emotionally based, inclusive framework. Ideally, multiple elements of value delivery through product/service branding, communications, and connection will come together to make this happen:

- Content—particularly video, which has grown in effectiveness and pervasiveness—which is relevant, informative, and objective, and available via multiple channels. Customers need to feel, and believe, that any information they are provided, and through whatever self-directed source, has personal benefit.
- Messaging produced by the organization must be consistent with content, seamlessly aligning with online and offline informal communication; and it should be recognized that decision making is (a) controlled by the customer and (b) likely to be influenced by both offline and online content and messaging.

Figure 2.1 A customer-centric culture

Source: Internet.

Sustaining trust, a foundation of customer centricity and value delivery, takes time and effort; and organizations need to recognize that the "bank account" of empathy, image, and reputation so carefully grown with customers can be wiped away virtually overnight. Contributing both directly and indirectly to building the customer behavior bank account is the value provided by employees.

Creating long-term customer loyalty and outstanding, memorable CX (and building this out to include employee loyalty and employee experience) means thinking about stakeholders in strategic relationship, rather than transactional, terms. This means that emotional drivers, sincerity, objectivity, and integrity, must come from inside the enterprise, including employee behavior and flexible processes. We address the specifics of employee emotional commitment later in the book. Bottom line at this point: To build bonding behavior, many organizations have created branded elements of the experience into their product/service value delivery; and, combined with the benefits of an endearing, customer-centric culture, they have gained the strategic financial rewards of true customer loyalty.

What Customer-Centric, Customer-Obsessed Companies Must Do

In building relationships with and value for customers, my longtime observation is that most organizations tend to progress through several stages of performance: customer awareness, customer sensitivity, customer focus, and customer obsession. As we demonstrate, these stages also apply equally to employees. And that is one of the insights we discuss, and hopefully embed, later in the book.

Here is the "executive summary" version of some conditions of each stage of enterprise customer focus:

1. *Basic customer (and employee) awareness*
   Customers are known, but in the aggregate. The organization believes it can select its customers and understand their needs. Measurement of performance is rudimentary, if it exists at all; and customer data are siloed. There's a traditional, hierarchical, top-down management

model, with "chimneyed" or "smokestack" communication (goes up or down, but not horizontal) with little evidence of teaming. Historically, this is also a basic, antecedent approach to employees applied by human resources.

2. *Enhanced customer (and employee) sensitivity*

Customers are known, but still mostly in the aggregate. Customer service is somewhat more evident (though still viewed as a cost center), with a focus on complaint and problem resolution (but not proactive complaint generation; internal groups tend to point fingers and blame each other for negative customer issues).

Measurement is mostly around customer attitudes and functional transactions, that is, satisfaction, with little awareness of emotional relationship drivers. The organization has a principally traditional, hierarchical, top-down management model, with "chimneyed" or "smokestack" communication (goes up or down, but not horizontal), with some evidence of teaming (mostly in areas of complaint resolution).

3. *Institutional customer (and employee) focus*

Customers are both known and valued, down to the individual level, and they are recognized as having different needs, both functional and emotional. The customer life cycle is front and center; and performance measurement is much more about emotion and value drivers than satisfaction. Service and value provision is regarded as an enterprise priority; and customer stabilization and recovery are goals when problems or complaints arise. Communication and collaboration with customers, between employees, and between employees and customers is featured. Management model and style is considerably more horizontal, with greater emphasis on teaming and employee contribution to improve customer value processes.

It's notable that, at this more evolved and advanced stage of enterprise customer centricity, complaints are thought of more in terms of a life cycle component, and recovery is more of a strategy than a resolution.

4. *Enterprisewide customer obsession*

Throughout the organization, customer needs and expectations—especially those that are emotional—are well understood, and response is appropriate (and often proactive).

Everyone is involved in providing value to customers—from C-suite to front line—and everyone understands his/her role. Customer behavior is recognized as essential to enterprise success, and optimal relationships are sought.

Performance measurement is focused, and shared, on what most monetizes customer behavior (loyalty, emotion, and communication metrics—such as brand bonding and advocacy—replace satisfaction and recommendation).

Customer service (along with pipelines and processes) is an enterprise priority and seen as a vital, and profitable, element of value delivery.

The management model is far more horizontal, replacing traditional hierarchy; and there is an emphasis on teaming, employee commitment, and inclusion of customers to create or enhance value.

Companies that are notably customer obsessed, and which makes them both unique and successful, have been extensively profiled by consultants and the business press. Often, they go so far as to create emotionally driven, engaged, and even branded experiences for their customers, strategically differentiating them from their peers.

CX consultant Ian Golding has outlined how culturally customer-centric companies can make value delivery a priority for the entire company:

1. **Talk about it**—If you want value delivery and CX to be a priority for everyone, then everyone needs to be talking about it as being so—from the CEO down to the front line and back up again. Talking about CX must be continuous and infinite if it is to remain a priority indefinitely.
2. **Show it**—If your organization has a vision (or mission) statement, it is imperative that you show how experience and value delivery is a priority for the company by making it one centered around the customer.
3. **Recruit for it**—If CX is going to be a priority for everyone, then you need to consider changing or implementing a recruitment policy that populates your organization with people whose own value systems are focused on customer centricity—this may also mean moving others

out of the organization who do not have customer-centric values. (Author note: Southwest Airlines, uniquely, utilizes panels of both current employees and Southwest travelers to interview prospective new hires. Only about 3 percent of prospective employees reaching this phase of the selection process are eventually hired).

4. **Create the conditions for it**—If you want your people to continuously THINK and ACT with the customer interests as a priority, then you need to enable and empower them to do what is right for the customer.

5. **Reward it**—Linking the performance objectives and remuneration of every single employee to the continuous improvement of CX is the most effective way of getting everyone in the organization to understand just how important it is. Making the rewards related to CX on a par with the rewards for achieving the businesses financial priorities makes this even more powerful.

As part of their overarching commitment to customers, these companies focus on the complete customer life cycle (and, as we will see, on the employee life cycle as well), and much more on retention, loyalty, and risk mitigation (and even winback, or customer recovery) than acquisition. (Figure 2.2) Support experiences are strategic, nimble, and seamless, and often omnichannel. In addition, there is emotionally felt "ownership" of an issue by employees when the customer experiences a problem.

For customer-obsessed companies, multiple sources of data are used to develop insights. Recognizing the information needs of their customers, they invest in altruistic content creation (over advertising); and they communicate proactively and in as personalized a manner as possible

Customer obsession, which can be referred to as "inside-out" customer centricity, has been a frequent subject of my blogs and articles: One of Albert Einstein's iconic quotes reflects the complete dedication of resources and values needed for an organization to optimize its relationships with customers: "Only one who devotes himself to a cause with his whole strength and soul can be a true master." Mastery requires, as well, a storehouse of experience coming from experimentation; so, just like in the pole vault and high jump, we can expect that the customer centricity bar will continue to be raised.

Suspect

Prospective customer

New customer

Retained/loyal/advocating customer

At-risk customer (attrition)

Lost customer (defection)

Recovered customer (won-back)

Figure 2.2 Seven customer life cycle stages

Source: Author.

As we will see, customer obsession also requires that organizations take a more stakeholder-centric approach to management and culture, putting greater emphasis on the role of employee experience, employee commitment, and employee contribution.

Improving the Basics: The New, and More Stakeholder-Centric, Customer Experience 4 Ps, and How They Impact the Employee Experience

In Marketing 101, everyone learns the basic four Ps of the classic "marketing mix," as defined by Neil Borden in the 1960s (Figure 2.3):

- Product—manufactured item or service
- Place—making the product or service accessible to customers
- Price—charging at a point above breakeven to make a profit
- Promotion—communicating to customers, prospects, and others about the product or service

Figure 2.3 The four Ps of marketing

Source: Internet.

Over the past 50 years, these four Ps have held up pretty well. After all, the product has to be right, be functionally sound, be durable, and work well. The price has to be right; and, even in the case of expensive durables or services, it has to be financially sound. The choice of place, reflective of distribution, communication, or purchase channel, must be in customers' hands at the right time. And, through promotion, the right target group or groups must receive needed communication about both the existence and availability of the product or service.

As sound as the four Ps have been, especially with respect to strategic deployment of marketing and other enterprise resources, changes in modes of communication and the move to greater customer focus within the enterprise have found customer behavior, and their loyalty to the brand/supplier, at growing risk. Companies have to be current with rising consumer expectations and need for personalized value. Digitization, for example, has made organizations become both transparent and accessible and has also increased the requirement that they become omnichannel in their contact strategy.

The traditional emphasis on functional touch points and transactional relationships has given way to a focus on overall CX that goes well beyond price-based commodity to greater innovation and relevance.

Today, we're dealing with a different, more nuanced value proposition landscape. The contemporary customer is more mobile, content seeking, impatient, and independent than at any time in history. Even with all of these new decision dynamics, the fundamentals of emotionally based trust and perceived value have become increasingly powerful drivers of customer loyalty and bonding.

As organizations become more customer centric, moving from what my colleague Colin Shaw defines as <u>naïve to natural</u>, or from simple and macro customer awareness, through greater sensitivity and focus, finally arriving at customer obsession, they will be well advised to add four new Ps to their toolbox:

Permeation—Dedication to providing optimized value must be absorbed into every nook and cranny of the organization, that is, board-room to mail room. Further, it must become core to shared enterprise values and superordinate goals and be an essential element of its cultural DNA.

Proaction—Organizations can no longer be content to just passively, tactically, and functionally react to customer needs and concerns. They must take the initiative and be committed to understanding what cus-tomers require as key value delivery elements.

For example, Chip Bell advises companies to give customers a "service souvenir," something both proactively offered and unexpected, that has attractive perceived value. Companies like Nordstrom actively do this. In one of Chip's blog posts, he quotes a Nordstrom employee saying how he adds to a customer's experience of value:

> If a customer buys a sports jacket, the obvious extension might be slacks or a tie. If you learn the customer is buying the jacket for a cruise, you might explore dressy shorts, an ascot, or a Panama hat. But, slipping a complimentary set of collar stays in the newly purchased jacket pocket (a frequently forgotten item on a trip) can leave a customer absolutely awed.

That cultural and process approach to customer value, called *lagniappe* by businesses in southern Louisiana (as part of the Creole service tradition) is *proaction* at work, and also a terrific story, which features an element of employee ambassadorship.

Partnering—Several years ago, James Unruh, former chairman and CEO of Unisys Corporation, said: "Partnering with customers promotes a deeper understanding of customer concerns and of areas for improve-ment. Partnering relationships can create a seamless interface between an organization and its customers." Smart and evolved companies create value in partnership with customers, and value is as likely to come from people and information/content as it is from products and services.

If companies practice ideas such as "creating interdependence" and "building equity" with their customers, they are strategically differentiating themselves from competitors and making it more difficult for their customers to leave and begin a relationship with a new supplier. And, the same thinking should be applied to the employee experience.

Paradigm—There are, to be sure, many ways in which an exemplary, world-class organization can be defined. From my perspective, it is an enterprise that creates trust, transparency, and confidence, especially in stakeholder (customer, employee, and supplier) experiences, and in reputation and image. These are critical to optimizing customer value delivery; and inherent in such cultures is the ambassadorial, trust-building behavior of employees (with customers and each other) and customer-forward processes.

The last P, *paradigm*, is especially important. It speaks to making customer centricity a paramount and lasting focus, of both a functional and an emotional relationship that exists between the enterprise and all of its stakeholders. Customer centricity, after all, is about more than structure, strategy, and systems. It's about the differentiation and engagement that lead to bonding between the organization and its stakeholders. It's about giving stakeholders greater enablement and empowerment, with a personal investment in the organization and its ongoing success.

It's about the enterprise becoming more transparent and open, connecting with customers through branded, emotional experiences and sustained value delivery, resulting in its operation as a "conscious capitalist." And, it is also about making customer centricity a platform for moving to stakeholder centricity, making sure that experience is a focus for initiatives and programs with both employees and customers.

Finally, paradigm is about "being human" as an organization, not just as a buzzword to apply to CX optimization. As Sisodia, Sheth, and Wolfe wrote in their classic customer centricity book *Firms of Endearment*:

What we call a humanistic company is run in such a way that its stakeholders—customers, employees, suppliers, etc.—develop an emotional connection with it. Humanistic companies seek to maximize their value to society as a whole, not just to their shareholders. They are the ultimate value creators. They create emotional value, experiential value, social value, and, of course, financial value.

Customers have shown strong desire to affiliate, and bond with, companies that are paradigmatic in providing unique, consistent, and value-based experiences. One of the key trends we're seeing in marketing is the greater ability of consumers to gather desired information and insight and interact directly with prospective vendors, much earlier in the prospecting and consideration process.

As can be seen from the following graphic (Figure 2.4), elements of prepurchase—awareness, interest, consideration, intent, and even evaluation—bring potential customers much more into direct contact with vendor employees. This presets emotions and memories that come actively into play later in the customer life cycle.

There's actually a fifth new P—*personalization*—that says more about the marketing mix as an extension of the stakeholder-centric enterprise. The most valuable customers appreciate and want more personalization and individualization, a relationship, and an emotional connection. It's up to organizations to (a) identify the strongest emotional drivers and (b) effectively leverage them.

Successful organizations have either morphed, or have begun to change for the better, by placing customers' and employees' interests and needs ahead of the enterprise's. They build a veritable bank account of trust; and there is ample evidence that high trust, and the positive

The new marketing and Sales Funnel

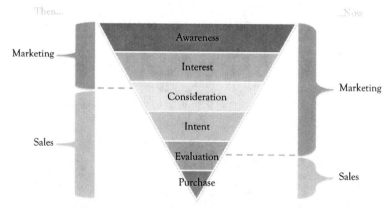

Figure 2.4 New marketing and sales funnel

Source: Internet.

reputation and image it breeds, is an enduring strategic advantage, a definite competitive differentiator. And, personalization truly optimizes the
customer and employee experience, perhaps its most important benefit.

Beyond Customer Centricity: Moving to a "People-First" Approach to Stakeholder Centricity

Arguably, one of the most culturally serious and financially significant
challenges facing companies today derives from the combined effects of
employee turnover and personal disengagement, which many academics
and customer research professionals believe link directly to suboptimal
customer marketplace behavior. Both are driven by organizations' and
staffs' levels of customer centricity and strategic focus.

Organizational customer centricity, identified as having a single, integrated view of customers and that required to create and sustain their
optimized behavior across the enterprise, cannot be created without
carefully managing staff loyalty, customer focus, and engagement. High
employee turnover, especially among frontline, customer-touching staff,
and low levels of customer-related productivity and proaction tend to
be nested within individual organizations' greater passivity and lack of
investment around concepts of "staff" and "customer" behavioral linkage.

Company culture and processes (principally visible in skills, values,
leadership, training, commitment and performance level, rewards and recognition, and both formal and informal communication) is a critical deter-
minant of both staff productivity and retention levels. For instance, the
U.S. Department of Labor's Bureau of Labor Statistics conducted a study
among 1,000 companies with 50 or more employees, and they have found
a negative correlation between an individual company's turnover and its
amount and type of staff training. Companies with low turnover rates spent
more than twice on training compared to those with high turnover rates.

Companies also have a spectrum of gauges to assess the various costs
associated with staff loyalty, productivity, and engagement. The "hard"
costs of employee turnover—newspaper advertising, recruiter fees, interviewing, medical exams, testing, moving allowances, and so on—have all
been well documented and quantified in detail. And, some of the "soft"
costs, such as:

(a) Time that managers and other employees spend finding, selecting, and interviewing potential replacements

(b) Personnel costs such as overtime pay and temporary help filling in for the missing employee, trainer and trainee time during the new employee's break-in period, and the cost of work put aside until the replacement is fully functional, not to mention

(c) The administrative and financial costs associated with departing employees have also been taken into consideration. Overall, basic hard and soft staff replacement costs have been estimated (by organizations such as Ernst & Young/Cap Gemini) at up to 150 percent, or more, of the departing employee's annual salary.

It is beginning to be understood, however, that the far more serious and strategic effect on corporate performance is the short-and long-term impact of employee turnover and disinterest on customer behavior, and it is there that relatively little is known, because, until quite recently, it has not been intensively studied or quantified.

Forbes, for example, has reported on how a people-first, stakeholder-centric culture is impacting both employees and how leaders interface with them. According to the Forbes Coaches Council, research from the University of Warwick has found that employees who identified as having a better experience were 12 percent more productive. So, when organizations invest in employee experience improvement, the result is a better bottom line and a more cohesive culture (Figure 2.5).

Figure 2.5 People-first stakeholder centricity

Source: Internet.

Stated in essential terms, people-first stakeholder centricity has enabled more and more companies to attract and retain desired employees and treat them the way that customers are treated. Members of the Forbes Coaches Council identified several factors that help define both the meaning and the benefits of a people-first culture:

- Creating greater loyalty and commitment. When employees feel that a sincere effort is being made to provide work that builds their passion, they will become stronger advocates for the organization.
- Attracting and keeping top talent more easily. When employees are empowered and enabled to be creative, they can be innovative.
- Contributing based on strengths and capabilities. When employees feel that they are performing in areas where they can excel, they will dive in, and perform better, even when it stretches their competencies.
- Younger employees want this. When employees, especially those under 35 years of age, see that the culture supports their desires to create, function as a team member, and build leadership skills, they make the organization more vital.
- Missions and goals can be made with greater speed. When employees see they are being led with their "why," rather than the manager's, they will help produce outstanding results.

There are a number of "markers" that characterize people-first, stakeholder-centric organizations, identified by senior HR executives who have looked into companies with these self-labeled cultures:

- "People first" is not only written into mission and vision statements, it is actively practiced.
- Senior executives behave in ways that support the culture.
- Trust is both given and earned in healthy organizations.
- Company success and growth are intertwined with a people-focused culture.
- There is flexibility in employee performance requirements and flexibility in company processes and procedures.

Of course, there can be impediments to both establishing and sustaining people-first cultures. Much of this has to do with HR's predisposition for conformity and dislike of uniqueness, the strong tendency to construct layers of employee management policies and procedures, the inability of rather soulless and antecedent employee behavior measurement approaches, and the marked proclivity to give priority to organizational needs over individual needs. Perhaps the biggest roadblock to becoming people-first is HR itself. The desire to key on employee fit, alignment, and productivity does not give employee experience or CX enough light to grow.

How does this change? First, HR has to become more forward thinking. Next, hard policies should be replaced by rules and policies. Third, employees should be more directly accountable and given more empowerment and permission to do their job, succeed, or fail. Finally, HR should become more focused on aligning individuals with their strengths, rather than forcing "fit" and "alignment." Culture change is serious business, requiring tremendous effort and discipline; but, that said, being people first is important and good for stakeholders and the enterprise.

One company that has functioned with a people-first approach from its inception is Ultimate Software (Figure 2.6), an organization with which we have been able to develop a close working relationship. As stated on the "Our Mission" page of Ultimate Software's website:

> Simply put, people are your company. They control everything—your products, your services, and how you separate yourselves from the competition. Make no mistake…it's your people that matter most to the success of your business. Winning companies put people first. If you focus on recruiting, cultivating, and retaining good people, you'll see better results. Period.

At Ultimate Software, based in Weston, Florida, "people first" is more than their attitude toward customers or the design of their products and services. It's a reflection of how the enterprise views the employee experience. As stated on their website's "Company Culture" page: "At Ultimate, we take care of our employees, and we know it will show in the way they take care of you."

Figure 2.6 Celebrating at Ultimate Software

Source: Ultimate Software Website.

Ultimate Software designs human capital management solutions for clients, and they also service what they sell. The culture is built on innovation, as well as respect, trust, and concern for optimizing the employee job experience. Another statement from the "Company Culture" page of their website reinforces this: "We take great pride in our people and their accomplishments, foster their continued professional growth, and encourage their ideas."

In a 2016 joint Beyond Philosophy–Ultimate Software webinar, Ultimate's approaches to employee experience were on display to hundreds of participants. First, they stated that according to an International Data Corporation (IDC) 2015 Experience Survey, 81 percent of U.S. companies measure CX in some form or fashion, while nearly 70 percent do not measure employee experience. Employee experience clearly needs greater priority within organizations today, and Ultimate Software has developed what they identify as an "Employee Experience Playbook" to address this. This experience model has three components:

- Leadership role (coaching, caring, inspiring) front and center, and well beyond traditional approaches to management. Leaders must ensure, for instance, that employees (a) feel connected to customers and (b) understand their role in optimizing CX.
- Culture of transparency, listening, trust, and action, which challenges employees, supports communication, and shows compassion. This is supported by analytics, which drives

understanding of the company's vision for customers, more positive employee perception of their contribution to customer success, and connection of employees to CX outcomes.

- Leverage technology as an "employee valet" to more efficiently complete tasks and contribute, supporting them so they can better communicate with customers and across the organization.

Ultimate Software truly practices people first, stressing meaningful work for employees, customer support, and value for all stakeholders. As a guiding principle, Ultimate has quoted noted leadership and management consultant Simon Sinek: "The employees must love the company before the customer ever will."

Becoming More Stakeholder Centric: Learning to Take Insightful Stock, Calculated Risk, and Positive Action

Today, there is a state of mind many of us enter at every year-end and year beginning. That state of mind is common to both individuals and enterprises, especially where true focus on CX optimization, employee performance, and stakeholder centricity are concerned. What should we be doing to appreciate and understand employees and customers better, to be more proactive, and to create more productive and real-world action in our decision making? For a little perspective on these questions, we can go back to 1982 and to Tom Peters and Robert Waterman's seminal business book *In Search of Excellence: Lessons From America's Best-Run Companies*.

Walking past for the moment the fact that, to some, the book's choice of 43 companies—NCR, Wang Labs, and others—appeared somewhat questionable (and that, in 2001, Peters "confessed" to *Fast Company* magazine that elements of their data had been "faked"), the book laid out eight themes, which identified excellent organizations and how they got, and stayed, that way. One of these, and perhaps the most important where attaining stakeholder centricity and customer advocacy behavior are concerned, was having a strong orientation, or bias, for getting things done.

In building and sustaining that bias for action, Peters and Waterman called for a reduction in organizational complexity, more aggressive review of problems, greater focus on learning and insight, and a move to *adhocracy*. Never heard of adhocracy? Long story short, adhocracy is an organizational theory and concept, first coined by Warren Bennis in 1968, which emphasizes the removal of bureaucracy in favor of a more flexible, organic, fluid, responsive, informal, and adaptive culture, structure, and customer-related processes.

There's a lot of creativity and innovation in such companies, especially where products, services, and customers are concerned; and, when initiatives are defined, programs and projects get done faster in adhocratic organizations. In companies that have reached the highest levels of customer centricity, or "natural" as we would define them, these organizations are also largely decentralized and horizontal and often obsessively focused on providing optimal customer value.

Organizational fluidity means there is a lot more informal and open communication, insight generation, data sharing, and MBWA (management by walking around). To help facilitate this desired fluidity, these companies tend to use more virtual technology for staying in contact. Anyone looking at how adhocratic companies operate would see a culture, which actively seeks out customer value opportunities, shares good and bad customer news, fragments responsibilities, leverages both ad hoc and permanent teams, and gives positive reinforcement for taking pathfinding, but considered, action.

Adhocratic, customer-centric companies not only have a bias for action, they seem to be endlessly experimenting, trying new ideas out, or as Peters and Waterman would say: "Do it, try it, fix it." These experiments, often quick in and quick out, are like the Manhattan Project, when the atomic bomb was developed during World War II—marked by focused leadership, management by objectives, individual accountability, use of concentrated data, building on success, and learning from "tries" and shortfalls.

At the end of the day (or the year), for many organizations, having a bias and an orientation for stakeholder-centric action, that is, do it, try it, fix it, means a shift in thinking, culture, structure, and operations. Companies less bold and daring will be at continuing risk. As Lee Iacocca famously said:

So what do we do? Anything. Something. So long as we just don't sit there. If we screw it up, start over. Try something else. If we wait until we've satisfied all the uncertainties, it may be too late.

He also said, as was quoted in Ford commercials: "Lead, follow or get out of the way." Companies with less of a bias for stakeholder-focused action will, increasingly, find themselves following or getting out of the way. In an uncertain world, that is pretty much a certainty.

CHAPTER 3

Challenges (and Opportunities) Represented by Focus on Employee Satisfaction and Engagement

Why, Oh Why, Is ANYBODY Still Thinking About, and Measuring, Satisfaction?

When *Customer Retention: An Integrated Process for Keeping Your Best Customers* (ASQ Press, Milwaukee, WI, 1995), my first book on customer behavior was published, now over 20 years ago, one of the strongest reactions voiced was the contention, and the proof offered, that satisfaction and performance that leads to retention were not only fundamentally different concepts and ways of thinking about customers, they also required different measurement protocols. Many felt that satisfaction and retention were the same. In reality, they are very, very discrete, conceptually and measurement-wise. Retention is about behavior or intended behavior, the motivation to remain a customer, whether at lower, equal, or higher purchase levels. Satisfaction is not about any of that.

Satisfaction has always been largely about short-term attitudes about a recent product or service experience. Attitudes are superficial and tactical, essentially dealing with transactions and interactions rather than longer-term experiences and relationships. It can sometimes be, as well, about behavioral intent, not behavior itself.

Satisfaction is also about the tangible, functional, and rational components of value (time/timeliness, accuracy, completeness, suitability, price, durability, functionality, etc.) and of value delivery. For decades, though, satisfaction has been a cornerstone of what we understand to be total quality in products and services, as perceived by the customer. Unfortunately, satisfaction has also been proven to have very little impact on, or connection to, actual customer behavior. I'd submit, with little risk of argument, that the hourglass sand on satisfaction meaning and actionability has finally run out.

Even total quality icon W. Edwards Deming believed that satisfaction was not an ineffective metric for understanding the impact of satisfaction on customer actions. In his book *Out of the Crisis* (MIT Press, Cambridge, MA, 1982, p. 141), Deming said:

> It will not suffice to have customers that are merely satisfied. An unhappy customer will switch. Unfortunately, a satisfied customer may also switch, on the theory that he could not lose much, and might gain. Profit in business comes from repeat customers, customers that boast about your product and service, and that bring friends with them. Fully allocated costs may well show that the profit in a transaction with a customer that comes back voluntarily may be 10 times the profit realized from a customer that responds to advertising and other persuasion.

This quote appeared in *Customer Retention* (p. 9). It's as true today; yet, in many companies, satisfaction remains the standard on which performance is judged.

When 35 years ago, Deming said, "Profit in business comes from repeat customers, customers that boast about your product and service, and that bring friends with them," he was talking about what, for the past decade, we have understood, and effectively measured and applied, as customer experience (CX) and customer advocacy behavior.

The satisfaction (and delight, Net Promoter Score [NPS], and Customer Effort Score [CES]) metric does not take emotionally based consumer brand favorability and volume/type of positive and negative online/offline word of mouth into consideration. And, as many consulting organizations have determined, today these factors are critical for both understanding and leveraging downstream customer behavior.

Advocacy and bonding, principally based on the kind of positive/ negative customer word of mouth and impression of the brand or vendor that Deming identified, has tremendous power and potential to create desired high-end customer behavior. Word of mouth, however, is a double-edged sword; and customers' negative communication, as much as praise, can have a damaging effect on other customers and noncustomers, as well as the communicating customer.

As a core performance metric, customer advocacy is very much alive and well in both b2b and b2c products and services. Scores of studies, in many verticals around the globe, have demonstrated that informal word of mouth and brand reputation/image are essential decision-making levers. If anything, due to the more critical nature of touch points, performance, brand perception, and relationships in b2b, bonding may well be more important in this arena than in the b2c world. Critically, in both b2b and b2c performance measurement, there is little evidence of metric flatlining or reaching an actionability plateau when advocacy measurement is used and socialized.

So, all of that said, is there a role for tangible quality, as measured by satisfaction, on customer behavior? And, what is the most actionable way to measure it? Based on extensive consulting, training, and research experience, in b2b and b2c verticals around the world, I'd suggest that much of tangibility is about the emotional and memorable underpinnings of trust and confidence these elements represent. As noted in many of my blog posts and white papers, an emotional subtext has been found to exist in all components of value delivery, whether tangible or intangible, whether transactional or experiential over time. Especially with regard to rational value elements, these basic "table stakes," when delivered to spec or as expected, will help drive trust, confidence, and future consideration. When the basics are not attained, underdelivery of basic tangible element will undermine trust and influence negative downstream behavior.

Some experiences are pleasurable in the subconscious, some are painful, some are superficial, some go deep. They can create sensations and feelings that can be a challenge to articulate, but that cause people to take action. Translating these subconscious emotions and feelings is the "holy grail" of customer journey design.

Seemingly forever, marketers and researchers have been trying to identify stable and predictable links between what consumers say about product and service experiences, what they mean, that is, the emotional and unconscious underpinnings about what they really think and believe, and what they do in terms of actual decision making and actions in the marketplace.

There is an intersection between CX with a product or service, internal reaction to that experience, informal peer-to-peer communication about the experience, and downstream customer decision making. It occurs in the personal emotional and subconscious distillation of that experience in creating memories forming the customer's behavior. This may sound a little technical and psychological for some, but reckoning with the meaning of emotional and subconscious response to experiences has important ramifications in the marketing world. It can mean knowing what customers really want, whether they will stay or leave a vendor, and whether they will be loyal brand advocates or not. We've come a long way from satisfaction.

As Ralph Poldervaart, a CX expert at the Beeckestijn Business School in the Netherlands has said: "Eighty to ninety percent of our (brand-related) behavior is determined by our subconscious mind." Everything about customers, customer behavior, and CX measurement discussed in this section applies equally to employees and employee experience. There is growing acceptance that stakeholders, as irrational and emotional beings, can't always accurately tell us what we need and want to know about their desires and how they make decisions. Research analysts and HRD professionals are just beginning to understand that this represents a sea change in how experience is both designed and interpreted.

Connecting Satisfaction with Behavior: Does the Service-Profit Chain (or Employee Engagement-Profit Chain) Still Work?

The Service-Profit Chain (Figure 3.1), an enterprise performance and financial results concept introduced by Gary Loveman, James Heskett, W. Earl Sasser, and Leonard Schlesinger in 1994 in the venerable *Harvard Business Review*, and in a 1997 book by the last three authors, can

The Service Profit Chain (Heskett, Sasser and Schlesinger, 1197)

Employees deliver the organisations' service concept or brand, which generates customer satisfaction, customer loyalty and ultimately, positive business outcomes

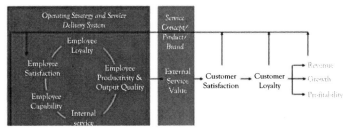

Figure 3.1 The Service-Profit Chain

Source: Internet rendering.

essentially be explained as follows: It is a theory of business management, which links employee satisfaction to customer loyalty and profitability. For the past two decades, it has been the analytical foundation used by many organizations to assess the health of their company.

More specifically, the Service-Profit Chain model makes a connection between high profits, customer loyalty and satisfaction, and employee productivity and satisfaction. In the model, customer satisfaction is derived from the value the customer receives from the company's satisfied and productive employees. Employee satisfaction comes from the support of corporate leaders who understand the needs of both employees and the customers. Employee satisfaction drives productivity, which, in turn, drives customer-perceived value. And, since new employees typically cannot provide a level of value as effectively as employees with tenure, the Service-Profit Chain also recognizes that employee retention directly impacts customer satisfaction. Thousands of organizations, and the executives leading them, have looked to the Service-Profit Chain model as a guiding star to help create enterprise success.

There is an ongoing, fundamental flaw with the Service-Profit Chain, not surfaced with much attention when the concept was first introduced or given much examination depth or frequency since that time. The reality is that its foundation of employee satisfaction leveraging both their actions and the actions of customers is built on shifting sand. Namely, the connection between satisfaction and behavior, whether by customers or employees, has been challenged and largely refuted in study upon study.

Here's a summary that encapsulates the difference between satisfaction and loyalty as metrics, expressed by Susan Wyse of Snap Surveys in a June 2012 post:

> Customer Satisfaction is a measurement of customer attitudes regarding products, services, and brands. Customer Loyalty on the other hand has two definitions. Customer Loyalty consists of loyalty behavior (also referred to as customer retention) which is the act of customers making repeat purchases of current brands, rather than choosing competitor brands. Secondly, Customer Loyalty encompasses loyalty attitudes which are opinions and feelings about products, services, brands, or businesses that are associated with repeat purchases.

So, while the line of thinking is somewhat incomplete, the key takeaways from Ms. Wyse's summary are (a) that satisfaction principally measures attitudes, which are passive, reactive, and tactical, and (b) that this metric has little connection to value-related behavior. Adding to the shortcomings associated with this metric and its application, satisfaction also tends to be what is known as a "lagging indicator," which will often decline faster following a negative experience than it will improve following a positive one.

What is true for customer attitudes relative to behavior can also be applied in equal measure to employees. Industrial psychologists and organizational behaviorists have been studying employee satisfaction for over 30 years, assuming that the level of staff satisfaction correlates with impact on measurable results. However, as one major study concluded: "Researchers have been unable to confirm a relationship between employee satisfaction and business performance."

This is almost identical to the oft-proven determination, of which Susan Wyse's explanation is one example, that a high level of customer satisfaction has relatively little bearing on loyalty behavior. And, for purposes of this discussion, it is the influence of employee satisfaction attitudes on customer behavior, which is at the core of the Service-Profit Chain's claimed linkage. Going the next step, beyond employee satisfaction, does their engagement profitably drive customer behavior?

First, what does employee engagement, which has been around for over 20 years, actually mean? Kevin Kruse, a former VP of Kenexa (now part of IBM) and a leadership contributor to *Forbes* magazine, defined employee engagement as "the emotional commitment the employee has to the organization and its goals." Note that Kruse's concept, like other ways that engagement is understood within HR circles, does not include any mention of customers, CX, or value delivery.

His perception of employee engagement, though it recognizes the power of emotional commitment, is simply another definitional iteration of many seen over the past two decades. They are almost entirely about alignment and productivity, and all make assumptions about the influence of engagement on customers.

Since first entering active HR use, employee engagement has had many meanings and interpretations, but relatively little of it has to do, by conceptual definition, specifically with impact on customer behavior. Thorough analysis conducted by The Conference Board in 2006 showed that among 12 leading engagement research companies, 26 key drivers of engagement could be identified, of which 8 were common to all:

- *Trust and integrity*—How well do managers communicate and "walk the talk"?
- *Nature of the job*—Is it mentally stimulating day to day?
- *Line of sight between employee performance and company performance*—Do employees understand how their work contributes to the company's performance?
- *Career growth opportunities*—Are there opportunities for growth within the company?
- *Pride about the company*—How much self-esteem do the employees feel by being associated with their company?
- *Co-workers*/team members—How much influence do they exert on the employee's level of engagement?
- *Employee development*—Is the company making an effort to develop the employee's skills?

- *Relationship with one's manager*—Does the employee value relationship(s) with manager(s), and is there trust and credibility between the levels?

Again, typically, there is little or no mention/inclusion of "customer," "customer focus," or "customer value" elements either in measurement or analysis of employee engagement. Though it is recognized that CX, and resultant behavior, can often be impacted by engagement, it is more tangential and inferential than purposeful in nature.

Kruse, whose definition of engagement comes close to the "line of sight" driver identified earlier, has created his own version of the Service-Profit Chain, as extended to employees, that is, the Engagement-Profit Chain, which, like the Service-Profit Chain, is built on creating customer satisfaction, rather than optimized employee experience or optimized customer experiences. He believes that engaged employees care more, are more productive, and use discretionary effort on behalf of the company's goals, which leads to:

- Higher service, quality, and productivity, which leads to…
- Higher customer satisfaction, which leads to…
- Increased sales (repeat business and referrals, defined as customer loyalty), which leads to…
- Higher levels of profit and growth, which leads to…
- Higher shareholder returns (i.e., stock price)

It's all very linear and very assumptive. In the article, Kruse flatly states: "Engaged employees lead to better business outcomes." Over 250,000 people have viewed his article, so it has had broad coverage. Like the Service-Profit Chain, the core flaw in the concept Kruse put forward in his thesis is that higher satisfaction, and even higher emotional commitment, by one stakeholder group, in this case employees, will drive the behavior of another stakeholder group, in this case customers. Unless the employee's emotional commitment (and reinforcement) is focused on customers, CX optimization, and product or service value delivery, there is likely to be only marginal-to-moderate influence on customer behavior. There isn't a straight line between employee engagement and customer behavior or corporate profitability.

The Value, and Limitation, of Building From a Base of Employee Engagement

Consulting organizations, and enterprises around the world, have been focused on understanding and leveraging drivers of employee engagement for close to 30 years. As a basis for generating greater employee fit, alignment, and productivity within macroorganizational goals, it works well. And, though not specifically designed to generate better employee experiences or to help deliver more positive and lasting value to customers, engagement has also proven to be an improvement and an advancement over employee satisfaction.

There is some excellent recent material that helps make this point. In a September 2016 post, entitled "Employee Engagement Primer," Bruce Temkin reviewed some of Temkin Group's research findings (*Employee Engagement Benchmark Study, 2016*) about the "virtuous cycle" employee engagement helps create. This model of engagement followed a pathway that began with Engaged Employees, moved to Great Customer Experiences (which moved to Loyal Customers, then Strong Financial Results, and then to Investment in Employees) and Lower Employee Turnover (which also moved to Strong Financial Results and then to Investment in Employees).

Loyal Customers, according to Temkin Group, then drove Prouder Employees, which led back to Employee Engagement. Again, this is a very linear, Manhattan Project-type, model of presumed results.

Some of the key findings, which Temkin Group believed make engaged employees a valuable asset include:

- Eighty-seven percent of highly engaged employees recommend their company's products and services, compared to only 21 percent of disengaged employees.
- Eighty-two percent of highly engaged employees do something that is good for their company, even if this is not expected, compared to only 19 percent of disengaged employees.
- Sixty percent of highly engaged employees make a recommendation about an improvement that can be made in their company, compared to only 15 percent of disengaged employees.

The same study also indicated that, based on the manner in which Temkin Group identified leading CX companies, those considered less effective in this area have only 49 percent highly/moderately engaged employees. Those companies considered more effective at CX, that is, the leaders, have 75 percent highly/moderately engaged employees.

Of course, to drive more positive CXs, the company first has to have engaged employees. According to Temkin Group's results from this study, only 25 percent of employees are considered highly engaged, and 31 percent are moderately engaged. One of the challenges associated with accepting that employee engagement can be considered the highest and most valuable level of the individual's behavior, vis-à-vis both employee experience and CX, is the metric or metrics used to measure it. In the Temkin Group's case, their Employee Engagement Index see Figure 3.2 is computed by a meld of the following three elements:

- I understand the overall mission of my company.
- My company asks for my feedback and acts upon my input.
- My company provides me with the training and the tools that I need to be successful.

What's missing from this index? As with virtually all known measures or models of employee engagement (other than Kevin Kruse's Employee Engagement-Profit Chain, discussed in the previous section), it is largely about alignment with mission and vision, communication, productivity, and the like. There is no mention of "customer," "customer experience," "value proposition," or any related terms.

In a study of 300 HR professionals in large North American organizations, Temkin Group found greater emphasis on employee training, recruiting and hiring, retaining key employees, employee engagement, and manager training. Wonderful, but what about employee experience and customer experience focus?

Customer-centric companies invariably have (and keep) employees who are invested and enthusiastic about optimizing CXs, whether they are frontline staff or not. While my inclination is to agree that engaged employees are more loyal to the organization than employees who are merely satisfied, and this also contributes to overall customer satisfaction,

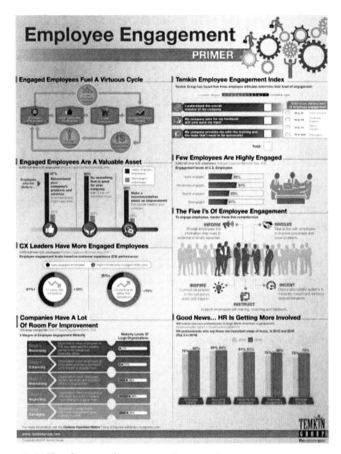

Figure 3.2 Temkin employee experience primer

Source: Customer Experience Matters, Temkin Group.

in my studies, a key finding is that there is only incidental correlation and causation between employee engagement and customer advocacy behavior. Employee ambassadorship is a different concept, where both purposeful employee commitment and CX optimization are emphasized.

Here's a section of one of my white papers, written a couple of years ago, addressing employee engagement:

> In the mid-1990's, more progressive companies had moved beyond employee satisfaction to employee engagement research. This was a significant step for human resources professionals. It was a recognition that companies needed to view employees not

only as a resource but also as partners in helping reach overall business goals. The principal intents of employee engagement, then, are to identify

- What originally drew individuals to the company
- What keeps them there
- What they see as their role and how involved they are in it
- How aligned they are with the company's goals and culture

Engagement seeks to quantify emotional and rational job satisfaction and motivation to think, feel, and act. This combination is extremely important for training, communication, staff management, and individual and group goal-setting. Engagement, however, represents a mélange of loosely related concepts, so it marginally impacts CX and downstream customer behavior.

Employee engagement, then, is principally about the individual's or group's fit, alignment, and productivity within the enterprise. It can be summarized as follows:

- **Commitment to company**—Commitment to, and being positive about, the company (through personal satisfaction, fulfillment, and an expression of pride), and to being a contributing, loyal, and fully aligned, member of the culture
- **Commitment to value proposition**—Commitment to, and alignment with, the mission and goals of the company, as expressed through perceived excellence (benefits and solutions) provided by products and/or services

Here is a graphic depiction (Figure 3.3) of how we can view employee engagement as a foundational thesis for understanding employee behavior.

What is largely absent from this thesis, of course, is focus on how employee emotions and behavior—wherever that employee is located within the enterprise—drives CX and also how it contributes to employee experience. In its 2015 Experience Survey, International Data Corporation (IDC) found that 81 percent of the organizations they studied

Employees That Score High on Commitment to the Company and
The Value Proposition Are Considered Engaged

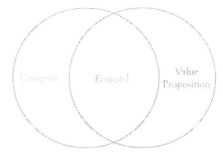

Figure 3.3 Employee engagement thesis

Source: Author.

measure CXs with their company; however, nearly 70 percent do not measure employee experience. This finding is somewhat mirrored and supported by electronic CX solutions company InMoment, with the finding that 70 percent of employee surveys do not include insights on how to improve the CX.

Contemporary approaches to employee engagement surveying include debriefing about customers and their experiences. This more expansive type of research, labeled voice of the employee, or VoE, studies, provide deeper looks into factors employees believe impact customer value delivery. As commented by InMoment's Paul Warner, vice president of consumer and employee insights:

> Over the nine years we've been collecting employee engagement feedback, we've heard from hundreds of thousands of employees across multiple industries and countries. In addition to talking about their own jobs, we found that nearly one-third of employees comment about the customer experience. Themes include ideas on how teams can work together better for the customer; how managers can better support employees when dealing with customers; and the barriers employees face in providing an exceptional experience. The sheer number of customer-centered comments is astounding. Even more interesting is that they emerge out of a process designed to gather their employees' perceptions of their own jobs—not necessarily the customer experience.

So, though this is indeed a VoE source and somewhat useful as an enhancement to employee engagement, it is principally anecdotal rather than dimensional insight. Warner added:

> Employees, especially front line staff, spend most of their time at the place where brand promise and customer experience meet. As such, they have a particularly empathetic view of customers, as well as inside knowledge of how and why your business works—and doesn't. Plus, inviting employees into improving and even designing better customer experiences enhances their own engagement levels. Companies that fail to leverage VoE to its fullest extent are leaving money on the table.

Ultimately, engagement studies are limited in their ability to directly link the employee experience to CX. As noted in an InMoment white paper, *Better CX Begins With Employees*, describing where VoE, employee engagement, and voice of the customer (VoC) intersect:

> While an employee engagement survey is a channel in which they can talk about how they view the company, its leaders, and their day-to-day experience, it is not the most effective way to gather data around how they view CX. In addition, employee engagement feedback is typically delivered to a human resources department charged with engaging the workforce, not improving customers' experiences.

There is a pervading thesis, around for decades, that more engaged employees lead to happier customers and that satisfied employees (who are, ipso facto, happy) equals engagement. And, it is there that the added value of employee ambassadorship, as a concept of emotionally based employee behavior and measurement framework, begins to become apparent.

The issue isn't—and never was—that engaged employees don't drive or leverage some degree of customer behavior. There's ample proof that this linkage exists. The issue is this: *Is there a better, more consistent, more effective, and globally actionable concept for both enhancing the employee experience and, contemporaneously, enhancing CX and value delivery?* The answer is yes, there is. It's ambassadorship; and the remainder of *Employee Ambassadorship* addresses its differences and its multiple, actionable benefits to enterprises and stakeholders. Employee ambassadorship is, as noted, a different concept, where both employee contribution and CX optimization are emphasized.

"U.S. Employee Engagement Reaches Three-Year High." Where CX and Value Delivery Are Concerned, Shouldn't We Ask: "So What?"

A recent article by a major employee research and engagement consulting organization led with the aforementioned headline. They were reporting on results of their national workforce tracking poll, the highlight of which was that employee engagement had risen 1.2 percent between January and February 2015 (to 32.9%) and that this new level was the highest engagement rate reported in the past three years.

The consulting organization went on to conclude from these findings that "recent trends suggest that improvements in engagement coincide with improvement in unemployment and underemployment," with the bottom-line summary statement that:

> A decline in the percentage of unemployed and underemployed Americans may have some influence on the percentage of engaged workers. As the job market becomes more competitive, it is possible that companies are putting more effort into engaging their current workers.

At best, this conclusion feels like a major s-t-r-e-t-c-h of correlation analysis results.

This same organization believes that "employee engagement is a leading indicator of future business success"; and to the degree that engagement level can impact staff turnover and productivity, both key contributors to profitability, this is a fair statement. However, when this organization, and others in the employee engagement research, training, and consultation space, make claims that engagement, in and of itself, contributes to customer value and loyalty behavior, two important questions need to be asked. Those questions are (1) Really? and (2) where's the consistent proof for individual companies?

Just as satisfaction has little proven connection to customer behavior, employee engagement was not designed to drive customer behavior. To build on this statement, let's begin by looking at the results of satisfaction on downstream customer action. Beyond extremely macroconnection to sales, customer satisfaction (as expressed through the American Customer Satisfaction Index [ACSI]) has been shown to have little direct connection to purchase behavior, to the tune of 0.0 to 0.1 percent correlation. Many companies are still measuring customer satisfaction in hopes that learning about its drivers will help build customer loyalty, but satisfaction isn't contemporary regarding decision making or reflective of what is going on in the customer's real, emotional world.

As noted, research and consulting organizations like Gallup, Parature, and BlessingWhite have determined that employee engagement can impact corporate profitability at the macrolevel (as much as three to four times higher for top-scoring engagement companies compared to those on the bottom half of companies using this measure); and that's one of the really valuable results it provides. A major 2012 collaborative secondary research effort, *Engage for Success*, by the University of Bath School of Management and Marks and Spencer in the United Kingdom concluded, as we've seen with other research into the benefits of employee engagement: "As well as performance and productivity, employee engagement impacts positively on levels of absenteeism, on retention, and on levels of innovation."

Where customer behavior changes are reported as a result of employee engagement, they were (like satisfaction's impact on customer behavior) also at macro and rather weak tea, incidental levels: "An earlier (2006) Gallup report that examined over 23,000 business units showed that companies with engagement levels in the top quartile averaged 12% higher customer advocacy than those in the bottom quartile." Like the "So what?" question, the consistent financial impact of engagement on individual companies and their customers, that is, on a microlevel, needs to be addressed, understood, and reported.

InMoment has determined that companies with high engagement scores have 2x the customer loyalty than companies with average employee engagement levels; however, the organization has also created a spectrum of employee perspectives and actions from passive to active engagement, where at the top, employees are more than loyal; they are advocates who will recommend their company to others. This top level is where engagement leaves off and ambassadorship begins.

Our view of employee advocacy, that is, ambassadorship, goes beyond recommendation. It includes strong commitment to the customers and company, and active, informal, vocal support for the organization and its products and services. Employee ambassadorship builds on the useful alignment and productivity represented by engagement; but, importantly, ambassadorship extends to include (a) the employees' perceptions about their influence on CX and (b) the linkage of employee experience and CX. Employee ambassadorship, or employee brand ambassadorship, has direct connections to—yet is distinctive from—both employee satisfaction and employee engagement as concepts and enterprise models.

Ambassadorial impact on customer behavior can be dramatic, extending the actions of employees to vocal support and commitment over and above experience value delivery. This goes beyond engagement. For example, InMoment has reported that companies in the top 25 percent of employee engagement outperformed the bottom 25 percent by 10 percent on customer ratings. Ambassadorship research findings, as will be shown, are significantly more positive and striking.

As a research framework, and method for understanding employee behavior, its overarching objective is to identify the most active and positive (and inactive and negative) level of employee commitment to the company's product and service value promise, to the company itself, and to optimizing CX. The ambassadorship thesis, with its component elements, that is, the three areas of commitment (two of which are identical to employee engagement), can thus be expressed as follows:

- **Commitment to company**—Commitment to, and being positive about, the company (through personal satisfaction, fulfillment, and an expression of pride), and to being a contributing, loyal, and fully aligned, member of the culture
- **Commitment to value proposition**—Commitment to, and alignment with, the mission and goals of the company, as

expressed through perceived excellence (benefits and solutions) provided by products and/or services

- **Commitment to customers**—Full commitment (by all employees and the enterprise) to understanding customer needs and to performing in a manner that provides customers with optimal experiences and relationships, as well as delivering the highest level of product and/or service value

Ambassadorship is linked to the key productivity and empowerment elements of employee satisfaction, engagement, and alignment research, and related training and operating approaches. However, it more directly contributes to business results, experience optimization, and value delivery because its key concept is building customer bonds through direct and indirect employee interaction, while, at the same time, enhancing the employee experience.

As companies strive to become more customer centric and stakeholder centric in all things they represent and do, we believe that the emphasis on building strong employee ambassadorship will continue to increase as a core objective.

CHAPTER 4

The Linkages Between Employee Commitment and the Customer Experience

Being Real with the Employee–Customer Connection

Several years ago, in worldwide customer service experience research conducted for a major high-tech organization, to help make them world-class providers and drive stronger downstream customer behavior, it was found that processes had to take service employees well beyond the basics of knowledge, efficiency, and friendliness. Consistently, and irrespective of continent or country (60 countries on 5 continents), the most effective reps showed true empathy and concern for the customer's issue, literally "owning" the issue as if it were theirs as well, walking in their customer's shoes, and making a true emotional connection.

Customer experience (CX) pros can argue back and forth about whether a vendor can create deep emotions and behaviors such as bonding and love in a customer. From my perspective, at least, experiences that drive customer brand trust and passion can be both shaped and sustained. That's largely a function of organizational culture, customer-focused processes—and employee ambassadorship. Ambassadorship builds both passion and partnership.

In Jeanne Bliss's great book *I Love You More Than My Dog: Five Decisions That Drive Extreme Customer Loyalty in Good Times and Bad*, she speaks to how companies can build deeper, more lasting emotional relationships. As Jeanne believes (with my enthusiastic agreement), "being real," with customers and employees is a key way more positively emotional, personal connections can be created. She says:

Companies that customers love work hard not to lose their personality—not in their products, not in their service, not in anything they do. They become beloved because of how they connect with customers in their lives. They relate personally with them. And their personalities come through during interaction with them.

One example she cites is The Container Store. The company is dedicated to creating transparency with employees, which, in turn, contributes to driving positive customer behavior. As she states: "By committing to creating an environment of trust and nurturing in their employees, The Container Store has successfully built a retail experience that compels customers to come back for more." There is a powerful connection between the employee experience and CX. As we've often noted, other organizations—Wegmans, Southwest Airlines, Zappos, USAA, WestJet, Trader Joe's, Umpqua Bank, Zane's Cycles, L.L. Bean, Disney, Harley-Davidson, Whole Foods Market—"get" this.

Employees are the synaptic connection in an organization's ability to optimize CX. Making the experience for customers personal, emotionally positive, distinctive, and attractive at each point where the company interacts with them requires an in-depth understanding of customer needs. It also requires a thorough understanding about what the company currently does to achieve that goal, particularly through employee behavior. It requires that companies understand, and leverage, the impact employees have on customer behavior at an emotional level (Figure 4.1).

As discussed earlier, employee satisfaction and engagement both have relatively passive and superficial linkage to customer personalization and perceived value, but employee ambassadorship and commitment will result in making each customer feel special (i.e., "the only girl in the world"). And this builds a stronger vendor–customer relationship and stronger financial performance on every key measure. And, by key measures, or key performance indicators (KPIs), we mean those that help understand and interpret the impact of subconscious response, emotion, and memory and their resulting effect on actionability and priorities for improvement.

Figure 4.1 Positive employees

Source: Internet.

Are Your CX KPIs Really "Key"?
Do They Include the Impact of Employees?

There was a recent line of discussion—"What is the optimal number of KPIs?"—in the CMO Network professional group on LinkedIn. The principal observation was that marketers put so many KPIs in place (and often confuse KPIs with metrics) that they become meaningless. So, there was a request for feedback from CMO Network members on what they felt was an optimum number.

As you might expect, because these are marketers, a variety of responses came back:

- Balanced approach, with some KPIs at a high level and some that are more granular
- Have just a few KPIs
- Have one or two KPIs
- Have three or four KPIs
- However many KPIs, make sure they are focused and aligned

So, this certainly could not be identified as unanimity of perspective within the ranks.

Going past the suggestion that individual KPIs and performance metrics are (or should be) somehow different, with disparate goals and objectives in application, the measure(s) question still remains an important one for any enterprise. From a stakeholder-centric, customer-centric, and CX management perspective, which is the "sweet spot" of organization and execution for any enterprise, we can begin with a blog that *Customer-Think* CEO Bob Thompson wrote almost a decade ago "Find the 'Ultimate' Loyalty Metric to Grow Your Business."

At base, the blog was a discussion of the use, and many challenges, of Net Promoter Score, or NPS, to identify drivers of business growth and a call to (a) keep surveys succinct, (b) recognize that there are other business objectives of merit (such as improving gross margins, net operating cash flow, and shareholder return), and (c) remind researchers, through the introduction of NPS, that they needed to be more practical.

In the blog, written on October 1, 2007, Thompson predicted that NPS would peak in the coming year, and then decline. It hasn't declined, even though the methodology and application of the KPI have been legitimately challenged (and even debunked) by many noted research professionals; and, in fact, if anything, NPS has managed to become more institutionalized, now being (questionably) extended as a method to measure employee behavior, a move some might identify as irrational annexation. Two of the key recommendations Thompson included in the blog were:

#5—Reward managers and employees for improving customer loyalty ... and (per Jeanne Bliss) ... drive change within the organization to "get people to work better together" serving customers.

#6—Plan to evolve and refine your measurements and rewards. You'll need to make adjustments over several years to keep it working just right.

Frankly, the evidence of experience in monitoring and working with many organizations has shown that relatively little of Thompson's great advice has been taken and applied. This is especially true where individual and team-based employee contribution to CX and customer behavior is concerned. With most companies still focused on measuring employee satisfaction, or happiness on the job, and engagement, which is principally about fit, productivity, and alignment, their impact on customer loyalty and advocacy rarely comes into the KPI discussion.

Bob Thompson's blog concluded with a reprise of the key message:

> Is there one "ultimate question" that will effectively measure customer loyalty for all businesses? The short answer: No. But the "ultimate answer" is that you must figure out the right metrics for your business. What is at stake is your customers' loyalty—and your future success.

Certainly, a key component of that success is the degree to which enhanced employee experience and employee commitment are created.

Beyond Engagement, Employee Commitment Significantly Impacts Customer Behavior: How Can Your Company and Customers Profit Most?

As stated in my writing for over a decade, a core personal and professional belief is that once an organization has framed (or reframed) the optimal emotional and rational components of value and CX, they would be well advised to apply the same broadened new-age thinking, and similar approaches, to the employee experience as well. For years, academic and professional studies have chronicled both the direct and indirect effect of employee commitment on customer behavior.

Today, there's a lot of discussion among corporate strategists, and even senior HR folks, about "putting employees first," such as Ultimate Software does (see Chapter 2). Whenever this is surfaced, and the operational proof of its real-time application is demonstrated, it's useful to ask some relevant questions with regard to ultimate "people-first" enterprise value, particularly where the employee experience vis-à-vis CX is concerned.

What takes precedence, or should take precedence, employees or customers? It's very much like other seminal questions: Which came first, cowboys or saloons? Chickens or eggs? While these last two important questions may never resolve, the role of employees in leveraging customer loyalty behavior is far simpler to understand.

It's impossible to have customer loyalty and advocacy without employees understanding their role as CX performance stakeholders. And, just as importantly, this extends to living the role, and behaving with full commitment, as value delivery agents and supplier ambassadors, inside and outside of the organization.

Satisfaction Is Almost Irrelevant

Employees are at least as important as other aspects of customer management in optimizing benefits for customers. They are key stakeholders in value delivery and brand/supplier success, and they frequently represent the difference between positive and negative experiences and whether customers stay or go.

The extent of their role and impact needs to be better understood, but as introduced earlier, employee satisfaction isn't the best way to do it. Why not? Industrial psychologists and organizational behaviorists have been studying employee satisfaction for more than 30 years. But, as noted earlier, they have been unable to confirm a sustainable, causative relationship between drivers of employee satisfaction and business performance.

More recently, researchers—including James Oakley of Purdue University, Northwestern University's Forum for People Performance Management and Measurement, and relationship experts Dwayne D. Gremler of Bowling Green State University and Kevin P. Gwinner of Kansas State University—have found that employee behavior and advocacy—regardless of the employee's level of satisfaction—have a direct and profound relationship with the behavior of customers, and also with corporate sales and profitability.

Employees are capable of directly contributing to both customer disappointment and customer delight. It is essential that companies have a research and analysis method that links staff experience and performance directly to customer behavior, so they can hire, train, recognize, and reward employees for how they contribute to customer value.

The Employee Ambassador

Companies must weigh the role and impact of employees, especially in creating benefit and value for customers. This is central to the employee experience as well as CX. When examining the leverage employees can exert on customer states of mind and brand decision making, a few companies have learned that employees loyal to the company are also loyal to its brands—and are more likely to act as ambassadors in creating customer commitment and advocacy.

A decade ago, two U.S. marketing professors, Eugene Fram of Rochester Institute of Technology and Michael McCarthy of Miami University, Ohio, reported on targeted employee behavior research conducted by The Conference Board. Among key results were that companies with employees who are highly loyal to their brands (i.e., commitment to the product and service value proposition) are more positive about their employment with the company itself; are more likely to believe the company is customer focused; and are more likely to have pride in the company and believe that it is well managed. (See "From Employee to Brand Champion" in the January–February 2003 issue of *Marketing Management*.) In fact, The Conference Board study results showed that 73 percent of higher brand loyalty employees had positive job experiences compared to only 41 percent with lower brand loyalty. The numbers Fram and McCarthy presented, shown in the following graphic (Figure 4.2), enumerate their findings.

The dual message here is that companies should focus greater attention both on creating brand "champions" and advocates among customers and on building these same capabilities within the job descriptions of all employees within the organization, irrespective of function or level.

(Important note: The results of early employee ambassadorship research, which are presented several chapters from now, showed even more positive percentage point differences on these measures, when those individuals identified as ambassadors through the framework we developed were compared to employees with lower levels of commitment behavior. For example, and recognizing that we are getting a bit ahead of ourselves, where Fram and McCarthy found a 20 percentage point difference between Low and High Brand Loyalty Employees on "Proud

Issues affecting employee brand loyalty (employees giving high attribute scores)			
	Lower Brand Loyalty Employees	Higher Brand Loyalty Employees	Percentage Point Difference
Employee product perceptions			
Greater number of features than competitor	28%	48%	+20
Higher overall quality than competitor	41%	73%	+32
Better overall value than competitor	38%	65%	+27
More prestigious than competitor	34%	58%	+24
Employee attitudes toward employer			
Proud to work for company	28%	48%	+20
Like working for company	41%	73%	+32
Company is well-managed	38%	65%	+27
Company is customer-focused	32%	59%	+27
Company promotion efforts			
Company encourages me to buy	22%	63%	+41
Company promotes or advertises to me	25%	54%	+29
Brand usage visibility			
Someone I live with sees what brand I use	54%	83%	+29
Someone I work with sees what brand I use	35%	53%	+18
Someone in my neighborhood sees what brand I use	21%	41%	+21

Figure 4.2 Issues affecting staff loyalty to employer and brand

Source: From "Employee to Brand Champion" in the January–February 2003 issue of *Marketing Management*.

to work for company," the difference between Employee saboteurs and Employee ambassadors was 64 percentage points. Higher differences between Low and High Brand Loyalty Employees and Employee saboteurs and Employee ambassadors also occurred, across the board, on all attitudes regarding aspects of the employer's products and services.)

How customers think and feel as a result of their touch and transactional experiences with suppliers links directly to subconscious responses created from employee mindset and behavior. These are the "moments of truth," and the emotions behind them, that drive what customers do downstream. Leading companies, such as Starbucks, deeply understand the importance of connecting emotionally with customers, and how brand value and employee behavior help achieve this. Starbucks CEO Howard Schultz has noted:

> The success of Starbucks demonstrates the fact we have built an emotional connection with our customers. I think we have a competitive advantage over classic brands in that every day we get to touch and interact with our customers directly.

Today, customers have more ways to engage with suppliers of goods and services than at any time in the past. So companies have more ways to succeed in creating a relationship—and also more ways to fail. Whether the "touch" is by paper, by a human being, or by electronic or mobile means, organizations must offer consistent, seamless, and positive experiences for customers. Service, especially, is often a major differentiator and lever for either customer advocacy or, if done grudgingly or poorly, customer defection.

Also important in gathering customer insights are employee feedback at key touch points so the company can know, in as real time as possible, what is working and what isn't. Finally, because these points of interaction are so critical in managing the overall experience—and frequently the key source of customer delight or pain—there must be a C-suite executive accountable and responsible for executing all of the touch point elements. Such an individual—let's call this person a chief customer officer, or CCO—has, until rather recently, been missing from the organization chart of many companies. Experts like my colleague Jeanne Bliss have done a great job in identifying the value and scope of contribution from these individuals; and we are seeing more companies adding a CCO to the ranks of senior executives.

My own research into the impact of delightful and disappointing CXs has shown that disappointing experiences will often lead directly to indifference in the relationship and engagement with a supplier. As customers become increasingly positive with their supplier experiences, and more emotionally bonded, this is the cause behind a direct correlation with advocacy levels. In fact, because of the strength of causation, the rate of correlation between the type of experience and degree of customer advocacy is almost 100 percent.

Increasingly, we are beginning to understand, and even predict, the effect on customer advocacy of employees. This is a "holy grail" for many organizations, as they strive to leverage human capital to best effect. As *Fortune* columnist Thomas Stewart said three decades ago, "Human beings want to pledge allegiance to something. The desire to belong is a foundation value, underlying all others" (*Fortune*, July 8, 1996).

When that "something" is the optimization of customer loyalty behavior, coupled with the highest levels of employee participation and investment in reaching that goal, all parties benefit. Employee experience, then, isn't necessarily a chicken-and-egg precursor to CX, but it is certainly parallel at minimum.

Employee Ambassadorship and Customer Advocacy: Delivering "Wow" Value Within the Enterprise

Because of my long-time strong interest in employee contribution to customer behavior, several years ago, as noted in the Employee Ambassador section, the need for a new research and analytical framework became evident to me. So, working with marketing scientists, we conducted research through a leading polling service among 4,300 U.S. adults who are employed full-time. Sample size was sufficient to provide baseline results in close to 20 major business and industry areas. More is discussed later in the book (Chapter 7 is almost entirely devoted to this), but we're introducing some of our key early insights here.

The questionnaire utilized for this study was constructed based on the "three legs" of the employee ambassadorship stool (commitment to company, commitment to value proposition, and commitment to customers), which is more thoroughly presented later in this chapter. So, the ambassadorship framework consisted of nine dependent attributes, or agree/disagree scale statements (three in each of the legs). In addition, a number of loyalty and advocacy (positive and negative communication and other behavior) metrics were used to help validate the employee ambassadorship framework.

Core to the original framework, we most typically concentrated on what drives active, positive, vocal commitment behavior and favorability about the company, that is, ambassadorship and advocacy; however, it was at least equally important to identify where employee indifference and negativism, potentially leading to cultural sabotage-type attitudes and actions, existed, why they existed, and how they could be mitigated or eliminated. If employee ambassadorship and advocacy represented the North Pole, then alienation and sabotage should be considered the South Pole.

Employees that scored high on these three behavioral and mindset components were considered ambassadors. Ambassadorship is linked to the productivity and empowerment elements of employee satisfaction, engagement, and alignment research; however, this behavior more closely correlated with business results and value building because its emphasis is building customer bonds through direct and indirect employee interaction.

In the research, about 15.5 percent of adults, employed full-time and working for a company, were identified through the framework as ambassadors. At the opposite end of the commitment spectrum about 29.5 percent qualified as saboteurs by their answers.

Several industry groups had ambassadorship and sabotage levels at approximately the same percentages as overall full-time employees:

- Education
- Health Care and Social Assistance
- Technology Services
- Banking and Finance
- Engineering Services
- Insurance

There were, as well, industry groups covered in the research with very high ambassadorship levels, coupled with low sabotage levels: Religious and Nonprofit organizations, Construction, and Legal Services. Conversely, there were industry groups with very low ambassadorship and high sabotage levels: Telecommunications, Retail Trade, Manufacturing, Transportation and Warehousing, and Accommodation and Food Services. It's interesting to note that, especially in telecom, retailing, lodging, and food services, these are some of the industries so often featured in business studies and trade stories and articles as representing the poorest reported CXs and highest levels of service complaint.

Some of our most consequential findings were as follows:

1. *Employee Loyalty*

   In addition to employee motivation, cohesion, productivity, and alignment with corporate values and culture, HR is perhaps most interested and focused on learning how to increase staff loyalty. Our research identified employee loyalty level through three specific metrics: rating of the organization as a place to work, likelihood to recommend the organization to friends or family members as a place to work (which some consulting organizations conflate with advocacy or ambassadorship), and level of felt loyalty to the organization. Overall, 18 percent of the respondents exhibited high loyalty to their organizations and 20 percent exhibited low loyalty; and, importantly, there were strong, almost polar opposite differences in organizational loyalty depending on whether an employee was categorized as an Ambassador or Saboteur:

   Low Employee Loyalty—19.8 percent (Total), 0.0 percent (Ambassador), 61.0 percent (Saboteur)

   Medium Employee Loyalty—61.9 percent (Total), 27.3 percent (Ambassador), 38.5 percent (Saboteur)

   High Employee Loyalty—18.3 percent (Total), 72.7 percent (Ambassador), 0.5 percent (Saboteur)

   These were definite "pay attention" findings for HR. It's a concern, of course, that almost 20 percent of employees have low organizational loyalty; however, it's an even greater challenge that there is three times the level of potential staff turnover among saboteurs, who, before they depart, will undermine and infect the performance and loyalty of other employees. Our research provided very specific insights into why this is occurring. At the same time, we suggested that the organization would be very well served to emulate the behaviors and attitudes of ambassadors through the rest of the culture.

2. *Vocal Commitment to the Company*

We determined that commitment to the company, in the form of loyalty and related attitudes and behaviors, is a fairly basic requirement for employee ambassadorship. As important is feeling that the company is both a good place to work and that its products and services are good, and communicating this belief to others, including colleagues, friends, and customers.

Similar to overall employee loyalty findings, ambassadors were found to be both positive and vocal promoters and representatives of the company as a place to work, while most saboteurs never, or less frequently, said anything good about the company as an employer. In terms of the highest frequency of saying positive things about the company as a place to be employed, ambassadors were over 40 times more likely to do this than saboteurs (85.7% compared to 2.1%):

Rarely/Never Say Positive Things About Employer—20.4 (Total), 0.9 percent (Ambassador), 55.5 percent (Saboteur)

Sometimes/Often Say Positive Things About Employer—49.6 percent (Total), 13.4 percent (Ambassador), 42.4 percent (Saboteur)

Almost Always/Always Say Positive Things About Employer—30.0 percent (Total), 85.7 percent (Ambassador), 2.1 percent (Saboteur)

When asked if they ever say anything bad about the company as a place to work, almost none of the ambassadors (1.9%) were frequent or occasional negative communicators in this regard. However, saboteurs were 26 times more likely to communicate to others in negative ways, either frequently or occasionally (49.4%). It's clear that this kind of attitude and behavior can have significant impact on attracting the best employees, keeping them, and having them be focused on customers.

3. *Vocal Commitment to Company Products/Services*

The third principal component of ambassadorship is representing the company's products and services, that is, its brand promise, to others, both inside and outside of the organization. Similar to their responses regarding the company as a place of employment, the disparity in saying good things about the company's products and services between ambassadors and saboteurs was dramatic: Over 20 times more, ambassadors always or almost always said positive things compared to saboteurs (78.3% vs. 3.7%).

Rarely/Never Say Products/Services Are Good—18.1 percent (Total), 1.6 percent (Ambassadors), 45.0 percent (Saboteurs)

Sometimes/Often Say Products/Services Are Good—54.1 percent (Total), 20.1 percent Ambassadors), 50.3 percent (Saboteurs)

Almost Always/Always Say Products/Services Are Good—27.8 percent (Total), 78 percent (Ambassadors), 3.7 percent (Saboteurs)

Saying negative things about the company's products or services was also significantly more prevalent among saboteurs, those employees who are truly alienated. Over 45 percent of employee saboteurs said negative things about products or services at least some of the time, compared to only 2.6 percent of ambassadors.

Again, we recommended that companies need to focus on the multi-layered consequences of such results. What actions should companies be taking with insights such as these? Here are several;

- Employees, at all levels and in all functions need to have a thorough understanding of what's important to customers so that their actions match customer expectations and require-ments.
- Employees' behavior needs to be aligned around CXs, and organizations should also focus on building the employee experience. Employee experience optimization should receive as much attention and focus as CX optimization.
- Build processes, technology, training, and management prac-tices that support employees being able to optimize CX.

Perhaps most of all, we felt that companies should evaluate the effec-tiveness of rules and metrics associated with delivering customer value. For instance, how effective is the company, and employees, at unearth-ing and resolving unexpressed complaints, which may be undermining customer loyalty? How are nonfinancial metrics viewed relative to financial ones? What types of automated support processes exist, and how well are employees trained in them, to make serving customers easier? How does the company balance taking care of existing customers, particularly those who may be at risk of defection, with acquiring new ones? How much cross-functional collaboration exists in support of the customer?

For companies to create and sustain higher levels of employee ambassadorship, it's necessary to have customer and employee intelligence specifically designed to close gaps between CX, outmoded internal beliefs, and rudimentary support and training. It's also essential that the employee experience be given as much emphasis as CX. If ambassadorship is to flourish, there must be value, and a sense of shared purpose, for the employee as well as the company and customer—in the form of recognition, reward (financial and training), and career opportunities.

Introduction to Examples of Employee Ambassadorship at Work

Companies like Virgin, Honeywell, TD Bank, NCR, ING, and Hewlett-Packard (HP) are actively creating and sustaining cultures of employee ambassadorship.

HP, for example, has a program called "Demo Days." All employees, those currently working for HP and also retired employees and irrespective of function or level within the organization, volunteer and are trained to spend days at local electronic retail stores, as brand ambassadors for the company, interacting with potential customers. HP does this several times a year, and it helps the organization build greater customer centricity into the culture.

At Zappos, the highly successful online footwear and clothing retailer, there's a strong belief that "your culture is your brand." During the hiring process, prospective employees, however talented and experienced, must fit into the culture. Following hiring, all employees—regardless of function or title—are trained in customer loyalty, service, and company values and vision over a four-week period. Two of those weeks are spent are spent on the phone, taking calls from customers.

Zappos has defined its company culture in terms of 10 core values, the first of which is "Deliver WOW Through Service." As summarized by CEO Tony Hsieh:

> Every employee can affect your company's brand, not just the front line employees that are paid to talk to your customers. It can be a positive influence, or a negative influence. We decided a long time ago that we didn't want our brand to be just about shoes, or clothing, or even online retailing. We decided that we wanted to build our brand to be about the very best customer service and the very best customer experience. We believe that customer service shouldn't be just a department, it should be the entire company. Our belief is that if you get the culture right, most of the other stuff—like great customer service, or building a great long-term brand, or passionate employees and customers—will happen naturally on its own.

Again, ambassadorship is most successful when employees are recognized and appreciated and can participate in the benefit and value they provide to customers. Whether an organization is a major international corporation, or a small, embryonic start-up, these words represent the spirit of what employee ambassadorship can accomplish for a company. Stated simply, ambassadorship is employees living the promise of "wow" customer value delivery, irrespective of whether they are interfacing with purchasers of the company's products and/or services, other colleagues, friends, or family members. It is also the partnership, and shared destiny, between employees and their employer. When this is done well, all stakeholders win.

Employee Retention, Engagement, and Ambassadorship Go Hand-in-Hand-in-Hand at Successful Companies

Nearly all companies are concerned about employee turnover; and, with the worldwide economy in recovery, it has become a priority. In some industries—notably retail, customer service, and hospitality—annual staff churn rates of 30 to 40 percent and more are not uncommon, and even considered acceptable. While this situation may be a reality in many companies, it isn't a very sound strategy, and from multiple perspectives:

- The value employees can bring to customers
- The breakdown in customer–staff continuity and trust when employees leave
- The negative cultural effect of turnover on other employees
- The real "total cost" of losing employees, including hiring, training/coaching, and productivity

So, retention, as well as contribution and cohesion, has become a huge issue today (see Figure 4.3). We should be concerned about it, of course; but we also need to focus on the degree to which employees who stay with a company are directly and indirectly contributing to customer loyalty behavior.

Numerous studies have been conducted on elements of employee value, addressing reward and recognition, job fit, career opportunities, work environment, departmental and management relationships, and so on. It is pretty much conventional wisdom that during this period where there is great demand for exceptional talent, especially individuals who are diligent, innovative, and customer focused, successful companies will also have loyal employees.

Figure 4.3 Employees pulling together for the company, the value proposition, and the customer

Source: Internet.

Ambassadorship is very definitely linked to the productivity and empowerment elements of employee satisfaction, engagement, and alignment research; however, it more closely parallels achievement of business results and value building because its emphasis is on strengthening customer bonds through direct and indirect employee interaction, as well as creating a stronger, more emotionally driven and rewarding employee experience.

Perhaps most of all, companies should evaluate the effectiveness of rules and metrics associated with delivering customer value. For instance, how effective is the company, and employee, at unearthing and resolving unexpressed complaints that may be undermining customer loyalty? How are nonfinancial metrics viewed relative to financial ones? What types of automated support processes exist, and how well are employees trained in them, to make serving customers easier? How does the company balance taking care of existing customers, particularly those who may be at risk of defection, with acquiring new ones? How much cross-functional collaboration exists in support of the customer?

For companies to create and sustain higher levels of employee ambassadorship, it's necessary to have customer and employee intelligence specifically designed to close gaps between CX, outmoded internal beliefs, and rudimentary support and training. It's also essential that the *employee experience*, especially vis-à-vis customers, be given as much emphasis as CX. If ambassadorship is to flourish, there must be value, and a sense of shared purpose, for the employee as well as the company and customer— in the form of recognition, reward (financial and training), and career opportunities.

With that in mind, consideration of employee impact should be actively reflected in how overall enterprise performance is measured.

There is a metric/KPI, or more appropriately a multiquestion framework (not an index) that will help sustain and continue to improve it. That framework is customer advocacy behavior: Advocacy is built on positive perception, active purchasing, and a strong and supportive vocal bond with a supplier, selected from all those that might be considered.

This type of customer behavior—where it comes from and how it can be leveraged—was outlined in my 2011 book *The Customer Advocate and The Customer Saboteur: Linking Social Word-of-Mouth, Brand*

Impression, and Stakeholder Behavior. A good portion of how customers behave toward, and bond with, a supplier has to do with employee commitment—to the company, to the product/service value proposition, and to the customers themselves. Employee commitment, which we define as ambassadorship, is a way of understanding customer effect that transcends both satisfaction and engagement. It directly influences customer advocacy.

One of the most useful, and granular, applications of customer advocacy measurement is that it can connect elements of employee behavior and brand value to CX. If, for example, a bank wanted to determine how much employees and brand equity were impacting customer loyalty, especially relative to the bank's key value proposition elements, this could readily be determined, per the following example (advocates are those who are vocal and positive, allegiants are those who are somewhat positive but minimally vocal, ambivalents are neutral and noncommunicative, alienateds are negative and vocal) (Figure 4.4).

Note that, not atypically, employee contribution to positive customer emotional response to experiences and transactions is, along with brand perception, stronger than key components of the value proposition itself. In our consulting and research assignments, we consistently see results such as these.

Here's the bottom line: There's nothing more powerful than linking causation with proof. That proof includes both employee-related and brand-related components. Extensive research in businesses around the world has demonstrated that a KPI, or metric, can be expressed as a single measure (as NPS originally postulated)—with the important proviso that it was drawn from an aggregated, relevant, and actionable (on a granular level) set of CX and behavior elements and drivers, not just a single, and questionable, question.

A Quick, Early Note About Designing Employee Studies and Interpreting Employee Research Data

In Chapter 7, we dive into the whys and wherefores of employee research; however, at this point, it is important to remember that, more than

Brand vs. Employee vs. Value proposition elements: connection to employee mindset/behavior				
Critical attributes	**(Scale: 1 to 10 agreement, 9 and 10 are top boxes)**			
Brand/Human	**Customer advocate**	**Allegiant customer**	**Ambivalent customer**	**Alienated customer**
Has earned my trust and confidence	81%	28%	6%	2%
It is a pleasure to do business with them	78%	22%	5%	1%
The bank is definitely for people like me	79%	26%	7%	2%
Bank employees				
Employees make me feel like a valued customer	75%	22%	8%	2%
Employees are trained to offer reliable services	71%	20%	7%	3%
Employees follow up with information as needed	71%	18%	5%	2%
Value proposition				
Breadth of checking and savings accounts offered	62%	13%	4%	1%
Variety of cards with different features suitable for me	53%	11%	4%	1%
Communication of different products and their features	60%	13%	3%	1%

Figure 4.4 Effect of brand, employees, and value proposition on bank customer behavior

Source: Author/Market Probe.

correlation, there must be a proven direct relationship between employee experience and CX for real actionability and morphing of the enterprise culture to take place.

For years, social scientists and consultants have warned the corporate world about making too much of correlation analysis, the simple regression technique that shows the relationship between one set of attitudes or behaviors and another. As an example, the "Service-Profit Chain," discussed in Chapter 3, is a model developed by three Harvard professors in the 90s, is generally summarized as happy employees = happy customers = happy shareholders.

In other words, at the core of effective employee engagement is the tacit belief that there is a direct relationship or linkage between higher employee satisfaction and CX. And, as found by noted CX expert Frank Capek, though elevated levels of customer service, and also increased profitability, may result from enhanced employee engagement:

> Just because employee satisfaction and engagement are correlated with customer satisfaction doesn't mean that making employees happier will lead to better customer experience. This is one of those classic traps your college professors warned you about: confusing correlation with causation. I've observed that this flaw in logic has led many organizations to invest in trying to make their employees happier in the hope that those happier employees will turn around and deliver a better experience for customers. We've just seen too many companies where, at best, more highly engaged employees simply deliver a sub-par experience more enthusiastically.

CHAPTER 5

Building to Employee Ambassadorship: Concept Scoping and Enterprise Value

How can companies keep a consistent customer focus and optimize business performance, which, after all, is the goal of customer centricity? Is it done with great products and product cocreation with customers? Is it through customer segmentation based on detailed profiling and interpretation? Or is it through outstanding service and original, effective marketing? Few would argue that all of these are important, of course; but, at the vast majority of companies, sales, service, and marketing functions and activities tend to be discrete. And, discrete, siloed execution equals suboptimized results.

There are many ways to bring all of these individual, rarely conjoined functions and capabilities into unison, so that they are more effective on behalf of both the customer and the employee. Perhaps the simplest, and arguably the most sustainable and strategically differentiated, is to have employees directly, actively involved in making this happen. OK, this—what we have labeled *employee ambassadorship*—is clearly a worthwhile goal, with two key and immediate questions: (1) How do you make this a reality, and (2) how do you measure the effectiveness of what you're doing? We'll address the second question first, and then offer examples of what companies like Virgin, Honeywell, Ford, NCR, ING, and Hewlett-Packard are doing to create and sustain a culture of employee ambassadorship.

A Culture of Customer "WOW" Begins with Employee Job Satisfaction. ...

As introduced earlier, the history of companies measuring employee job satisfaction, and endeavoring to link employee perceptions with customer behavior goes back almost 100 years. Organizational surveys began during the 1920s and 1930s, a result of emphasis on industrial engineering and time-and-motion studies, which began at the dawn of the 20th century.

By the 1960s and 1970s, many companies were conducting *employee attitude and satisfaction* studies; and these studies were further refined during the 1980s and early 1990s, focused as much on achieving quality as on creating satisfied employees. It has long been found, however, that talented and motivated employees expect more from companies. For these employees, job satisfaction includes a different set of criteria. They want to be enabled and empowered. They want to be challenged and pushed. They want their work to have real meaning. They want personal and professional development opportunities so they can grow and advance their careers.

The problem with employee satisfaction is that it does not focus on the things that are important to your most talented staff. A happy or content employee might be quite satisfied with a job that requires very little effort. This employee might be perfectly content doing the bare minimum required to keep his or her job. These employees are likely "very satisfied" with their jobs. They are unlikely to leave the company, but they are not necessarily adding value. Companies began to recognize that, as a company, if they focused on increasing the wrong kind of employee satisfaction, they risked entrenching those employees who are adding the least value, and for whom personal experience was the least important, while driving their most talented employees out.

... Is Enhanced Through Employee Alignment with the Company's Mission and Brand Promise. ...

In the mid-1990s, more progressive companies had moved on to *employee engagement* research. This was a significant step for human resources professionals. It was a recognition that companies needed to view employees not only as a resource but also as partners in helping reach overall business goals. The principal intents of employee engagement, then, are to identify:

- What originally drew individuals to the company
- What keeps them there
- What they see as their overall and day-to-day role and how involved they are in it
- How aligned they are with the company's, vision, mission, goals, and culture

Engagement seeks to quantify emotional and rational job satisfaction and motivation to think, feel, and act in the company's best interests. This combination is extremely important for training, communication, staff management, and individual and group goal setting. But, though engagement does drive both employee behavior and has some linkage to customer behavior, these results are more incidental by-products of the HR-based goals of fit, alignment, and productivity.

Brand engagement is an extension of employee engagement. Much of brand engagement is managed through the marketing structure, and it involves the communication of company values, and product and service benefits, to current and potential customers and to other stakeholders. Some companies have recognized that to deliver the brand promise externally, employees represent the biggest opportunity to arrive at that destination. Involving employees more directly in brand building has definite advantages for HR, such as attracting and retaining good employees, and creating a stronger understanding of the company's mission and vision, which then combine to build a more cohesive and aligned work force.

Employees, whether they are customer facing or not, need to "live" the brand and company value promise as company representatives, both inside and outside of the organization. Concepts and programs such as employee engagement and brand engagement (through employees), though considerably more progressive than job satisfaction initiatives, can be less than sufficient to help companies optimize the customer experience (CX) or sustain top-level customer value delivery. Employees may believe they are doing valuable things for their company and/or they may have positive feelings about their jobs, their employers, and the brands they represent; but, where is the specificity around building the best CX and relationships?

As discussed, in its basic thesis, engagement loosely parallels the "Service-Profit Chain," a model developed by Heskett, Sasser, and Schlesinger[1] in the 1990s. The model is generally summarized as *happy employees* = *happy customers* = *happy shareholders.* In other words, at the core of engagement is the tacit belief that there is a direct relationship or linkage, that is, correlation, between higher employee satisfaction and CX.

One of the shortfalls too often seen in engagement, particularly as this type of research applies to optimizing CX, is that even if employees are trained in brand image, this does not mean they will deliver on the product or service value promise to customers or other stakeholders. Image needs to be integrated with building a culture of true customer focus. In other words, the external brand promise has to be experienced by customers every time they interact with the company.

... And Culminates in Ambassadorship, Where Employees "Live" the Brand Promise, for Themselves and for the Benefit and Loyalty Behavior of Customers

Can companies, through employee research, learn how to prioritize initiatives, which will generate optimum staff commitment to the company, to the brand value promise, and to the customers?

If employee satisfaction and employee engagement aren't specifically designed to meet this critical objective, and only tangentially correlate with customer behavior, can a single technique provide the means to do that? The answer to both questions is *yes,* through employee ambassadorship research. Employee ambassadorship has been specifically designed to both build on employee satisfaction and engagement and bring the customer into the equation, linking employee attitudes and actions to customer loyalty behavior.

To build on the concept and thesis begun earlier in the book, applying employee ambassadorship, or employee brand ambassadorship, has direct

---

[1] Heskett, J.L., W.E. Sasser, L.A. Schlesinger. 1997. The Service Profit Chain. New York City: Free Press/Simon & Schuster.

connections to—yet is distinctive from—both employee satisfaction and employee engagement. As a research and operating framework, its overarching objective is to identify the most active and positive (and inactive and negative) level of employee commitment to the company's product and service value promise, to the company itself, and to optimizing CX.

Ambassadorship is very definitely linked to the productivity and empowerment elements of employee satisfaction, engagement, and alignment research; however, it more closely parallels achievement of business results and value building because its emphasis is on strengthening customer bonds through direct and indirect employee interaction.

(**Note:** Recognizing that some companies are still focused on alignment and engagement, and also that there are many ways in which it can be expressed through employee research, we define employee engagement as encompassing two of the three components of our definition of ambassadorship. These are *commitment to company* and *commitment to value proposition*. Operationally, these are addressed in surveys through six of the nine *proprietary* questions we use in ambassadorship, which are discussed in Chapter 7).

Commitment to the company, in the form of loyalty and related attitudes and behaviors, is a fairly basic requirement for employee ambassadorship. As important is feeling that the company is a good place to work, and that its products and services are good, and communicating this belief to others, including colleagues, friends, and customers (Figure 5.1).

For companies to create and sustain higher levels of employee ambassadorship, it's necessary to have customer and employee intelligence

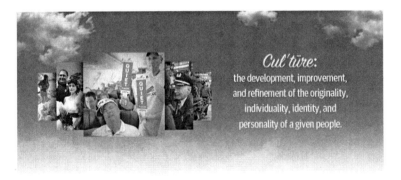

Figure 5.1 Stakeholder-centric ambassadorial culture

Source: Internet.

specifically designed to close gaps between CX, outmoded internal beliefs, and rudimentary support and training. It's also essential that the *employee experience* be given as much emphasis as CX. If ambassadorship is to flourish, there must be value, and a sense of shared purpose, for the employee as well as the company and customer—in the form of recognition, reward (financial and training), and career opportunities.

Multiple Benefits of Being Human with Stakeholders

Recent corporate performance results, from an evaluation focusing on the trend of more proactive and inclusive stakeholder approaches, now approaching "buzz concept" model status, of enterprises representing positive human characteristics—higher purpose, social responsibility, trust and honesty, altruism, inclusiveness, being values driven, and so on—for all stakeholders:

A key opportunity for companies to become stronger, more trusted, and more viable to customers and employees is creation of branded experiences. Beyond simply selling a product or service, these "experiential brands" connect with their customers. They understand that delivering on the tangible and functional elements of value are just table stakes, and that really connecting, and having an emotionally based relationship, with customers is the key to leveraging loyalty and advocacy behavior.

These companies are also invariably quite disciplined and proactive. Every aspect of a company's offering—customer service, advertising, packaging, billing, products, and so on—are all thought out for consistency. They market, and create experiences, within the branded vision. IKEA might get away with selling superexpensive furniture, but they don't. Starbucks might make more money selling Pepsi, but they don't. Every function that delivers experience is "closed loop" and 360 degree, carefully maintaining a balance between customer expectations and what is actually executed.

In his 2010 book *Marketing 3.0: From Products to Customers to the Human Spirit*, noted marketing scholar Philip Kotler recognized that the new model for organizations was to treat customers not as mere consumers but as the complex, multidimensional human beings that they are.

Customers, in turn, have been choosing companies and products that satisfy deeper needs for participation, creativity, community, and idealism.

This sea change is why, according to Kotler, the future of marketing will be in creating products, services, and company cultures that inspire, include, and reflect the values of target customers as well as employees. It also means that every transaction and touch point interaction, and the long-term relationship, needed to carry forward the organization's unique character, must be a reflection of the perceived value represented to the customer.

Kotler picked up a theme that was articulated in the 2007 book *Firms of Endearment*. Authors Jagdish Sheth, Raj Sisodia, and Daniel B. Wolfe labeled such organizations "humanistic" companies, that is, those which seek to maximize their value to each group of stakeholders, not just to shareholders. As they stated, right up-front (Chapter 1, page 4):

> What we call a humanistic company is run in such a way that its stakeholders—customers, employees, suppliers, business partners, society, and many investors—develop an emotional connection with it, an affectionate regard not unlike the way many people feel about their favorite sports teams. Humanistic companies— or firms of endearment (FoEs)—seek to maximize their value to society as a whole, not just to their shareholders. They are the ultimate value creators: They create emotional value, experiential value, social value, and of course, financial value. People who interact with such companies feel safe, secure, and pleased in their dealings. They enjoy working with or for the company, buying from it, investing in it, and having it as a neighbor.

For these authors, a truly great company is one that makes the world a better place because it exists. It's as simple as that. In the book, they have identified about 30 companies, from multiple industries, that met their criteria. They included CarMax, BMW, Costco, Harley-Davidson, IKEA, JetBlue, Johnson & Johnson, New Balance, Patagonia, Timberland, Trader Joe's, UPS, Wegmans, and Southwest Airlines. Had the book been written a bit later, it's likely that Zappos would have made their list as well.

The authors compared financial performance of their selections with the 11 public companies identified by Jim Collins in *Good to Great: Why Some Companies Make the Leap...And Others Don't* as superior in terms of investor return over an extended period of time. Here's what Sheth and his colleagues learned:

- Over a 10-year horizon, their selected companies outper- formed the Good to Great companies by 1,028 to 331 percent (a 3.1 to 1 ratio).
- Over five years, their selected companies outperformed the Good to Great companies by 128 to 77 percent (a 1.7 to 1 ratio).

Just on the basis of comparison to the S&P 500, the public com- panies singled out by *Firms of Endearment* returned 1,026 percent for investors over the 10 years ending June 30, 2006, compared to 122 percent for the S&P 500, more than an 8 to 1 ratio. Over 5 years, it was even higher—128 percent compared to 13 percent, about a 10 to 1 ratio.

Bottom line: Being human is good for the balance sheet as well as stakeholders. As Southwest Airlines founder Herb Kelleher has observed, "A humanistic approach to business can pay handsome dividends, even in a somewhat benighted industry like air passenger service."

Exemplars of branded CX also understand that there is a "journey" for customers in relationships with preferred companies. It begins with awareness, how the brand is introduced, that is, the promise. Then, prom- ise and created expectations must at least equal—and, ideally, exceed— real-world touch point results (such as through service), initially and sustained over time, with a minimum of disappointment.

As noted, there is a strong recognition that customer service is espe- cially important in the branded experience. Service is one of the few times that companies will directly interact with their customers. This interac- tion helps the company understand customers' needs while, at the same time, shaping customers' overall perception of the company and influenc- ing both downstream communication and future purchase.

And, branding CX requires that the brand's image, its personality if you will, is sustained and reinforced in communications and in every point of contact. Advanced companies map and plan this out, recognizing that experiences are actually a form of branding architecture, brought to life through excellent engineering. Companies need to focus on the touch points, which are most impactful, that is, which drive emotional response, memory, and downstream behavior.

Also, how much influence do your employees have on customer value perceptions and loyalty behavior through their day-to-day interactions? All employees, whether they are customer facing or not, are the key common denominator in delivering optimized branded CXs. Making the experience for customers positive and attractive at each point where the company interacts with them requires an in-depth understanding of both customer needs and what the company currently does to achieve that goal, particularly through the employees. That means that companies must fully comprehend, and leverage, the impact employees have on customer behavior. Employee proaction and teamwork are clearly critical here.

So, is your company "human"? Does it focus on providing stakeholder benefit? Does it understand customers, and their individual journeys? Are CXs "human" and branded? Is communication, and are marketing efforts, omnichannel, microsegmented, and even personalized? Does the company create an emotional, trust-based connection and relationships with customers and with employees as well? If the answer to these questions is Yes, then "being human" becomes a reality, the value of which has been recognized for some time, and not merely a buzz concept.

If picking current and well-researched books on this general topic, my first selection would be *Conscious Capitalism, With a New Preface by the Authors: Liberating the Heroic Spirit of* Business, a treatment of this trend by Raj Sisodia (coauthor of *Firms of Endearment*, Wharton School Publishing, 2007) and John Mackey, co-CEO of Whole Foods Market. In addition to organizations like Whole Foods Market, the Conscious Capitalism "movement" includes senior executives from companies like Southwest Airlines, Costco, Google, Bazaarvoice, First United Bank, The Container Store, Patagonia, UPS, Trader Joe's, and dozens of others.

As stated in their book,

> Conscious Capitalism is a way of thinking about capitalism and business that better reflects where we are in the human journey, the state of our world today, and the innate potential of business to have a positive impact on the world. Conscious businesses are galvanized by higher purposes that serve, align, and integrate the interests of all their major stakeholders.

This sounds reasonable, even high-minded; but, does it monetize?

Mackey and Sisodia have directly addressed this issue, that is, how well the conscious capitalism firms have fared financially, in their book (see pp. 277–278). Not surprisingly, conscious capitalism is also good business. They looked at the investment performances of the Firms of Endearment (FoE) companies versus the Standard & Poor's (S&P) 500 during the period from 1996 through 2011. Here's what they found:

Return rate
Fifteen years
FoE—1,646 percent cumulative, 21 percent annualized
S&P 500—157 percent cumulative, 6.5 percent annualized
Ten years
FoE—254 percent cumulative, 13.5 percent annualized
S&P 500—30.7 percent cumulative, 2.7 percent annualized
Five years
FoE—56.4 percent cumulative, 9.4 percent annualized
S&P 500—15.6 percent cumulative, 2.9 percent annualized

For those who are skeptical about the superior performance of values-based, more customer-centric and "human" approaches representing exceptional returns, and believe that taking a longer view is needed to provide more assurance, it should be recognized that the 2006-to-2011 period includes both the financial meltdown and the slow recovery. Unlike Net Promoter Score (NPS), which was suspicious from the beginning because of the limited number of examples offered, the results of close to 30 selected companies were evaluated by Sheth, Sisodia and Wolfe in their book. These companies not only significantly outperformed

Collins's *Good to Great* companies (which he chose because they had delivered cumulative returns at least three times greater than the market over a 15-year period), but also, over time, they monetized extremely well on an individual, collective, and cumulative basis.

In *Firms of Endearment*, it was noted by the authors that none of the Good to Great companies were selected for their list. For instance, Altria (the parent company of Philip Morris and John Middleton) performed well and made Collins's list, but didn't make the FoE cut because, viewed on a societal level, the company represented diminished value. This thesis is straightforward and easy to understand, whether you are a tree hugger or not.

Sisodia used the same FoE companies in the new results quoted in *Conscious Capitalism*, which, because it was published this year, represents the most current available financial results.

So, even in the challenging economic times represented by the past five years, enterprises living human approaches to stakeholder value delivery still perform at over 3x the S&P 500. I can't speak for everybody's definition of effective financial performance, but this is good enough for me.

An Example of Conscious Capitalism and Unconscious Capitalism

All of the changes in customer decision-making dynamics and influences on corporate and brand perception over the past decade or two have brought b2b and b2c marketplaces to a new frontier. There is an increasingly critical connection between brand promise, corporate trustability and reputation, CX as created by people and processes, and downstream customer behavior.

In an exploding Newtonian way, any small ripple in reputation change (such as through a product recall, operating scandal, or executive miscue), brand performance, or customer service can have a tsunami-type effect. And the "long-tail" of online social media may make the damage last indefinitely. Employees have a particularly important role here. Studies have found that employees are often less than enthusiastic about their employers and the goods they produce. As noted in many discussions of employee ambassadorship, small lapses in committed behavior by employees, identified as "badvocacy" by Weber Shandwick, can cause a great deal of damage to enterprise reputations and business outcomes. Negative or ambivalent employee attitude often drives customer complaints, some of which are expressed and some of which are either suppressed, mentioned in casual conversation, or posted on social media sites.

Enter Wells Fargo, and its admitted multiyear illegal sales practices across the company, first reported in mid-September 2016—although, with all of the media attention, including widely covered congressional hearings, it felt like the situation had been going on for years. After findings that many accounts had been falsified (such as creating fake e-mail addresses) or forced on unsuspecting customers, netting the company billions of dollars in profits, Wells Fargo paid a (relatively small) $185 million fine to regulators.

In a September 13, 2016 *Wall Street Journal* article, CEO John Stumpf said that the bank didn't have a bad culture, but that it has been working to weed out bad employee behavior. As he'd stated, "Everything we do is built on trust. It doesn't happen with one transaction, in one day on the job or in one quarter. It's earned relationship by relationship." Pronouncements like that should reflect a customer-centric culture, ambassadorial employee behavior, and positive customer perception. At Wells Fargo, it can be argued that none of these existed as a result of their actions. Instead, Stumpf has said that the problems were caused by "rogue" employees, 5,300 of whom were fired over a several-year period. These employees were principally nonmanagerial bankers and lower-level supervisors.

Massive employee dismissal is reflective of a disturbing business trend, where corporate executives lay the blame on staff for various negative customer value situations, rather than on cultural chinks. Like other recent, very public value–diminishing customer events, such as incurred by United Air Lines, Comcast, FedEx, General Motors, Toyota, and others, the Wells Fargo story may be with us for some time. Though Stumpf has said that "I'm thinking about how do we move forward," his testimony before the Senate Banking Committee did little to help with doing that. And, in fact, he has been forced out (though he'll pick up over $100 million in severance). As commented by comedian John Oliver, what Stumpf and his weak defenses of the Wells Fargo scandal have disclosed are issues of corrupt enterprise DNA and failed leadership.

On September 8, 2016, Stumpf had sent a message to all Wells Fargo employees, the day the news of the massive fraud was breaking.

In it, he referred to the Wells Fargo culture multiple times, saying, "Our entire culture is centered on doing what is right for our customers." A week later, in the *Wall Street Journal* article referenced earlier, he directly blamed employees, saying, "There was no incentive to do bad things." These are the words of an out-of-touch leader, reflecting an incoherent and nontransparent stakeholder culture. Particularly evident in the Wells Fargo reporting was the emerging operational and cultural disconnect, which has existed between senior and middle management, and between lower-level supervisory and nonmanagerial employees. A more real-world description of what Wells Fargo's customers have experienced came from John Shrewsberry, the CFO, who has said that the bank's issues were principally due to "people trying to meet minimum goals to hang onto their job." If the massive pressure for cross selling by the rank-and-file Wells Fargo employees isn't a mirror reflection of a stakeholder-insensitive, values-absent culture, what is?

If there is agreement on goals and values between levels of employees within an organization, the good news is that people generally trust those that they work with every day. Unfortunately, per a recent survey done by the London Business School and MIT's Sloan School of Management, the bad news, as can occur in a large company like Wells Fargo, was that senior management trusts junior management or nonmanagement only about 10 percent of the time.

Junior managers, supervisors, and nonmanagers often couldn't identify many of the organization's major priorities, leaving a vacuum and lack of clarity. Result: more direct pressure and close supervision from above, a minimum of nonmanager and first-line supervisor enablement and empowerment, and an impaired employee experience. It's pretty clear that this combination of factors represents, over an extended period of time, what has brought Wells Fargo to this unfortunate position (Figure 5.2). Time will tell how long it takes senior leaders, the remaining employees, and customers, to recover their former levels of trust.

There is, of course, a prescriptive to rebuild Wells Fargo's culture, and it begins with addressing drivers of stakeholder experience from the inside out. Wells Fargo has recognized this, and its new advertising both apologizes for past practices and promises to make things right for all stakeholders. It reflects sensitivity promises to both customers and employees.

Figure 5.2 Wells Fargo, an example of unconscious capitalism

Source: Internet.

But, they will need to do more. As my colleague Colin Shaw noted in one of his posts:

> Wells Fargo talks about eliminating product sales goals for their retail banking team. An essential step to creating a customer-focused culture is to change your Key Performance Indicators (KPIs). As global customer experience consultants, we say that KPIs tied to your sales goals influence the culture to focus on its goals rather than on what the customer needs or wants. Same concept follows for incentives. If people get paid to sell more products, they will sell more products. Before you judge foolish Wells Fargo, remember that product sales goals are a KPI that most organizations employ. Chances are that your company is making the same mistake that Wells Fargo is; it just hasn't imploded on you. Yet.

And, by extension, this prescriptive will not be successful until it extends to employees and the employee experience.

One of my favorite models for doing this is Baptist Health Care, based in Pensacola, Florida. Baptist, simply, has one of the most progressive stakeholder-centric, value and values-driven, cultures to be found anywhere in the world (Figure 5.3). Here are some of the things I'd written about the organization from a few years ago:

Figure 5.3 Baptist Hospital (part of Baptist Health Care), an example of conscious capitalism

Source: Baptist Health Care website.

There's a culture of inclusion and participation at BHC which employees desire and appreciate. Money's always a part of the value employees see in their job, to be sure; but, it's the environment, training, plus the daily and long-term experience, that are so much more important to them. At Baptist, employees respect each other's professions. It's well understood, for instance, that nurses are the direct link to the patients. They're at the bedside, the first line of patient-employee contact, like customer service reps. In a shared value and climate of "patients come first," everyone pulls together. That's a central reason why BHC's rate of staff turnover continues to go down.

Employees want enrichment. They want communication and participation. They want training. They want recognition. They want to have pride in where they work. They want management to lead by example. At Baptist Health Care, this all exists; and the benefits of a stakeholder- and customer-centric culture are realities that everyone can see, everyday. If customer-centricity can be created in healthcare, it can be created anywhere.

Baptist doesn't have rogue employees. They have a corps, and teams, of brand ambassadors. Baptist doesn't have name-and-blame executives.

They have servant leaders. Baptist doesn't have a repressive, high-pressure culture. They have trust and stakeholder centricity. Baptist Health Care is a leader in its industry. The Wells Fargo board did not allow John Stumpf to remain as CEO, and for new CEO Tim Sloan, perhaps a near-term trip to Pensacola to enlist in Baptist as an "outside culture expert" would be a useful way to begin moving forward.

Summing Up, What's the Value of Ambassadorship for the Company, the Customer, and the Employee?

In August 2004, Honeywell International Inc.'s chairman and CEO at the time, David Cole, sent a message to the company's 120,000+ employees, in which he described their role in the company's program to build and protect their brands:

> Every Honeywell employee is a brand ambassador. With every customer contact and whenever we represent Honeywell, we have the opportunity either to strengthen the Honeywell name or to cause it to lose some of its luster and prestige. Generations of Honeywell employees have built our powerful brands with their hard work, spirit of innovation, passion for quality, and commitment to customers. I am counting on every Honeywell employee to continue that legacy.

Again, ambassadorship is most successful when employees are recognized and appreciated and can participate in the benefit and value they provide to customers. Hal Rosenbluth, former CEO of the highly successful, multibillion-dollar travel management company, Rosenbluth International (which is now part of American Express Travel Related Services), said in the book coauthored with Diane Peters, *The Customer Comes Second*:

> We're talking about a change that puts the people in organizations above everything else. They are cared for, valued, empowered, and motivated to care for their clients. When a company puts its

people first, the results are spectacular. Their people are inspired to provide a level of service that truly comes from the heart. It can't be faked. Companies are only fooling themselves when they believe that "The Customer Comes First." People do not inherently put the customer first, and they certainly don't do it because their employer expects it. We're not saying choose your people over your customers. We're saying focus on your people because of your customers. That way, everybody wins.

Whether an organization is a major international corporation or a small, embryonic start-up, these words represent the spirit of what employee ambassadorship can accomplish for a company. Stated simply, ambassadorship is employees living the promise of "wow" customer value delivery, irrespective of whether they are interfacing with purchasers of the company's products and/or services, other colleagues, friends, or family members. It is also the partnership, and shared destiny, between employees and their employer. When this is done well, all stakeholders win.

CHAPTER 6

Customers and Employees, and the Emotional Drivers They Share As Stakeholders

Why Customer and Employee Experience Focus Has Morphed (or Needs to Morph) from Cognitive and Rational to Emotional and Relationship Driven

Over the past 30 years, much of customer and employee research has focused almost entirely on the cognitive, rational, and functional elements of decision making and behavior. Why? Well, researchers are (mostly) logical, and the cognitive and rational certainly looks logical—and emotions, or emotional context within the enterprise culture, can be challenging to measure.

Employee research progress has lagged behind the more progressive approaches to understanding customer value and behavior drivers. For years, especially in qualitative research, professionals endeavored to get at employee "feelings" involved when making job-related decisions, but that didn't help very much. As noted by Sigal Barsade and Olivia O'Neill in a recent *Harvard Business Review* article "Manage Your Emotional Culture" (January–February, 2016), "Most companies pay little attention to how employees are—or should be—feeling. They don't realize how central emotions are to building the right culture."

When asking things like career path, that is, future with the organization, the approach had always been to identify importance, or level of expectation, based on what the employee has thus far experienced on the job. These are expressed desires and needs, and there is a profound difference between what job elements employees say are priorities, what they mean, and what results in actual behaviors.

Much of employee and customer experience (CX) research still does this—getting stated importance (through techniques like conjoint analysis and MaxDiff) and attribute ratings, identifying choices, and using modeling techniques to estimate decision weights—but, at the end of the day, it, that is, largely cognitive and rational qual and quant, doesn't work very well. In customer research, even when looking at product and service features that appear strictly rational, there is often an emotional underpinning. In other words, emotions are driving these importance and performance ratings; and their impact on customer (or employee) experience perception needs to be understood.

The sea change that occurred in marketing over the past decade, that is the movement from push to pull, has been profound. The consumer now has access to both formal and informal (online and offline word of mouth and other socially based) information. Consumers are actively generating their own content; and this shift in decision-making control has forced concomitant change among corporations and researchers. It has, in the process, also created an awareness that stakeholder emotions must be more actively considered.

And, to parallel this trend, academics were actively studying the impact of emotions on various types of perception and decision making. There has been a great deal of this, on subjects ranging from metaphor elicitation to emotional and personalized weight processing. Daniel Kahneman's book *Thinking, Fast and Slow* has been especially important for researchers as they endeavor to understand how subconscious emotions and memory impact decision making and behavior. As my colleague Howard Lax stated in a recent post on the importance of emotions:

Emotions create connections or 'hooks' that people can and will recall. Emotions give meaning to experiences and make them more relevant to our lives. The more meaning we attach to an experience, the more importance we give it, the more likely it is that we will feel emotionally connected in some way and the more likely that we will remember it. Experiences that don't stir emotions simply have less meaning for us, making them more likely to be forgotten. The bland is inherently forgettable, like tasteless food and white noise.

Perhaps the most seminal impact of the new focus on emotions and memory is that they play a role not only in trust, favorability, and relationship elements of the individual's experience but on the more basic tangible components of value delivery as well. Things that, as researchers, we always considered to be the functional and rational elements of experience—price, accuracy, completeness, consistency, reliability, ease of use, and so on—have an emotional, often memorable, base that must be considered. Newer emotional measurement techniques actively incorporate valence, that is, sentiment, which clusters emotions into the positive drivers of advocacy, negative drivers of disaffection, and neutral drivers of ambivalence. We see a lot of this, for example, in such current applications as text analytics.

Specifically, researchers are keying in on the eight basic emotions—fear, trust, joy, anticipation, anger, disgust, sadness, and surprise—and organizing them to identify impact, individually and collectively, on decision making. And, for each basic emotion, there are shadings of greater or lesser intensity—serenity (lesser) and excitement (greater) for joy, grief (greater) and pensiveness (lesser) for sadness, and so on—and quasi emotional and relationship states that fall in between the basics, such as awe and disapproval, which fall on either side of surprise. Love falls in between joy and trust. It's emotional, of course, but it makes sense in application.

There is a recognition that stakeholders have a right to be happy, framing how they interpret experiences to help meet that goal. Behavioral science plays a big role here. Consulting organizations like McKinsey have reported extensively on the design of experience and how behavioral science can help improve stakeholder response. Work can be challenging and stressful. Like customers, employees can experience low-to-high psychological discomfort when faced with unexpected changes, and this can directly impact their perception of experiences.

Academic researchers like Professor Richard Chase at the University of Southern California's Marshall School of Business have used research on how people develop perspectives about their experiences to design more stability and reduce discomfort.

For example, psychologically we know that human fear is unpleasant, can range from terror (greater) to apprehension (lesser), creates very direct (and negative) impression, and causes people to retreat or withdraw. If

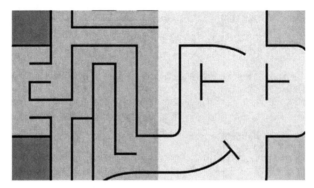

Figure 6.1 Behavioral science: pathways through the stakeholder's mind

Source: Internet.

negative elements of experience can be minimized, especially at the outset, emotions and memories of the experience will be more positive. All of the remaining seven core emotions we have discussed have similar relationships. This can be applied to a lot of what we need to understand about CXs and the overall customer journey.

Trust, however, may be the most important emotion, flanked by acceptance (lesser) and admiration (greater). It has much to do with response to brand image and reputation, which, along with core functional elements of the experience, is a key driver of customer decision making. Trust is also the most fragile of emotions, and can easily compromise a relationship.

What is clear in all of this Figure 6.1 is that consumers behave with a broad range of emotions, usually complex, in their brand and product journeys. At each stage of a customer's life, the researcher needs tools that will help interpret the meaning of emotions like anticipation at the prospect and initial purchase phase of the customer life cycle, and joy or anger, once the purchase or service experience has been completed.

For everyone involved with customers and employees, understanding and endeavoring to manage their behavior will never be the same. It's a brave, somewhat scary, new, emotionally driven world for experience researchers. Everyone, especially those involved in interpreting decision behavior drivers, should strap in and get used to it.

Building Stakeholder-Centric, Trust-Based Relationships

More than a buzzword, "being human," especially in brand building and leveraging customer relationships, has become a buzz phrase or buzz concept. But, there is little that is new or trailblazing in this idea. To understand customers, the enterprise needs to think in human, emotional terms. To make the brand or company more attractive, and have more impact on customer decision making, there must be an emphasis on creating more perceived value and more personalization. Much of this is, culturally, operationally, and from a communications perspective, what we have been describing as "inside-out advocacy" for years.

Most brands and corporations get by on transactional approaches to customer relationships. These might include customer service speed, occasional price promotions, merchandising gimmicks, new product offerings, and the like. In most instances, the customers see no brand "personality" or brand-to-brand differentiation, and their experience of the brand is one-dimensional, easily capable of replacement. Moreover, the customer has no personal investment in choosing, and staying with, one brand or supplier over another.

Thinking About Stakeholder Emotions, and How to Build Positivism

Early in the book, we introduced a hierarchy of emotional value, utilized to build stronger and more lasting stakeholder experiences. As the model showed, all emotions are geared to drive long-term experiential value. However, some of them—irritation, neglect, dissatisfaction, stress, disappointment, and frustration—destroy positivism. The emotions driving advocacy and ambassadorial behavior include trust, value, safety, cared for, and pleased.

One of the most frequent ways HRD has historically used to help build employee positivism is through reward and recognition programs. For generations, organizations have sought to leverage these kinds of initiatives to incentivize and sustain stronger individual performance.

It is well understood that employee commitment is built on their personal experiences and also their view of the future. Employees need to have confidence in management and the direction of the enterprise with respect to delivering value. Not unimportantly, this impacts employee perception of learning and career advancement opportunities, as well as how they are seen as people, and how they are appreciated within the company. Reward and recognition help to shape these perceptions.

In HRD circles, it's generally understood that there are significant differences between reward and recognition. Multiple studies have determined that nonmonetary rewards and individual recognition can drive more positive behavior than compensation, and over a long period of time. Still, organizations are wise to consider something of a "total rewards perspective," whereby programs have both tangible and intangible elements.

Recently, Hay Group conducted a survey in partnership with WorldatWork, a global compensation and work–life association, to see how (not if) these programs influenced positive employee behavior. The study, among 650 reward professionals, found that, from their perspective, short-term incentives and bonus programs, along with benefits and perquisites, are considered the most impactful motivators. That said, these reward pros saw nonintangible elements of reward programs (nature of the job, quality of work environment, career development, and driving toward more of a work–life balance) as having greater long-term effect. In other words, it was really the impact on employee experience that was key.

WorldatWork has also looked at the array of employee reward programs and practices. A study of close to 1,500 reward professionals showed that companies of all sizes and in all industries were predominantly using performance-based pay increases and variable pay approaches (commissions, retention bonuses, individual performance-based incentives, and hiring bonuses). But, at equal or higher rates, companies were applying informal recognition (manager/peer appreciation, spontaneous celebration, major life/family event acknowledgment, etc.) approaches. Large companies also frequently had more formal recognition programs, such as employee of the month, length of service, employee suggestion, safety performance, and so on.

Other studies have shown that a focus on reward, as contrasted with recognition, can (1) increase the negative culture of competition and name-and-blame, rather than collaboration and teamwork and (2) create an environment where employees are focusing more on specific outcomes associated with the rewards, partially or completely neglecting other areas of performance. Neither of these situations is desirable from either an employee or a CX perspective.

So, as long as they are meaningful and not superficial, intrinsic recognition programs can significantly help with employee ambassadorship goals. They can increase employees' sense of personal competence and worth, resulting in increased pride in their work and the on-the-job experience. They can build both meaningfulness and purpose for the employee, helping clarify and emphasize their role within the overall organization. And, for the organization, recognition programs can help reinforce shared values and vision, and improve teamwork and cultural cohesion.

How effective can they be at increasing commitment and loyalty and decreasing unhappiness and ineffectiveness? Here are some great statistics from Globoforce:

- The products of recognition programs—career opportunities and organizational reputation—are high behavioral drivers (Aon Hewitt).
- The #1 reason most Americans leave their jobs is because they don't feel appreciated, and this undercuts the job experience. Two-thirds of people surveyed said they received no recognition for good work in the past year (Gallup).
- Companies with strategic recognition programs have close to 30 percent lower employee frustration levels than those without such programs (Society for Human Resource Management [SHRM]).
- Organizations with effective recognition programs had one-third lower voluntary turnover than those with ineffective programs (Bersin by Deloitte); similarly, SHRM reported that companies with strategic recognition programs had mean employee turnover rates one-quarter lower than those without such programs.

- Almost half of the companies that use peer-to-peer recognition have seen marked increases in customer satisfaction (SHRM).
- Management praise and commendation was rated the top motivator for performance by two-thirds of employees, significantly higher than other noncash or financial incentives (McKinsey).

Employee tenure awards, identified in the preceding text, are perhaps among the most pervasive of these programs. According to an Engage-2Excel report, their recent studies indicate that close to 80 percent of all U.S. companies have formal length-of-service programs.

Overwhelmingly (74%) employees believe that these programs make employees feel more valued and appreciated. This was even higher among 24- to 34-year-olds and employees with less than 10 years of tenure. There was a drop-off with 11+ years of tenure and among older (45+) employees.

Also, the more senior and more educated an employee, the more favorably these programs were viewed. There were, it should be noted, gender differences: Seventy-seven percent of men feel the programs are effective, compared to only 64 percent of women.

Length-of-service recognition programs were most prevalent in banking (88%), retail and wholesale food industry (85%), and various forms of manufacturing (80%). They were least evident in education (70%) and restaurants (65%). There was also a prevalence for larger organizations to have formal service recognition programs.

What is clear from studies such as those done by Engage2Excel, is that these tenure recognition programs have a profound and positive effect on employee perceptions and behavior. Not only do these programs make employees feel more valued, they translate into commitment and loyalty behavior.

Some organizations invest considerably more time and attention on the onboarding and early training processes and put far less attention on creating commitment and involvement over time (perhaps assuming that seasoned employees will just settle into the culture and have the same level of enthusiasm as they did at the outset).

We have seen these programs and perspectives taken to extremes, and in less than positive ways. One of our clients openly welcomed new hires into the company fold, while, simultaneously, neglecting to appropriately recognize and reward tenure. In our research, we found that employees with over one year of tenure were considerably less committed and connected on virtually all aspects of their on-the-job experience and with other groups within the organization.

Specifically, after the first 11 months with this employer, employees were more often reflecting emotions, which were decidedly more negative—feeling stressed, hurried, and frustrated. At over 5 years, and continuing over 10 years, commitment dramatically declined. We discuss this more thoroughly in the next chapter.

While individual loyalty and personal commitment to the company's success remained high; however, belief in the quality of the company's products and services declined over time. Critical areas of experience, such as leadership, customer focus, training, advancement, environment, teamwork, and business alignment trended lower after 10 years of employment. Job satisfaction and likelihood to remain with the company also diminished. While there were multiple areas of tenure-related impact, the most significant (and eye opening to our client) declines were in perception of the fairness and consistency of selection processes for promotion and feeling that they have low involvement in decisions impacting their work.

Perhaps most instructive and insightful about the findings had little to do with the results themselves. It was that, by their own admission, the HR management of our client admitted that in all the years they have been conducting employee engagement research, none of the emotional and tenure-related issues had ever been surfaced, much less found to be so critical to the employee experience. (Note: We provide even greater depth on this research, and the value of insights it offers, in Chapter 7.)

So, it's clear: The subconscious, emotional, and memory aspects of the employee experience drive the most value. Without a sense of purpose, and reward and recognition built around the employee's commitment and delivery of value, much of the employee's contribution to the enterprise can be impacted.

In this example, as in much of the employee research we have conducted, it is the subconscious emotionally driven challenges that exist in key, core areas such as advancement (salary, career, changing employee experience needs, promotion selection process, and so on) and bonding (using employee feedback, being involved in decisions impacting work, enjoying relationships with co-workers, and so on). They (a) often haven't been previously identified by HR in the past through employee engagement research and (b) need to be addressed and prioritized, for the sake of stakeholder centricity, emotional positivism, and employee experience optimization.

A Universal Emotion for All Stakeholders: Love Makes the World Go Around

Creating value and generating optimized loyalty behavior, have a lot in common with love. Building from the song "Love Is a Many Splendored Thing" (recently celebrating its 60th anniversary, having been recorded by Philly group The Four Aces in 1955), perceived value and marketplace behavior are the result of experience(s), which, whether tangible or relationship based, influence emotion and leave elements of memory. Memory shapes impression and trust, leading to action. It's a lot like love, leading to a (hopefully) lasting relationship.

Flash forward to the movie *Moulin Rouge*, where Christian once again quotes the Beatles song title, and adds: "Love is like oxygen. All you need is love." Experience is the oxygen (or the nitrogen) that feeds the array of emotional responses, the most powerful of which stay in the stakeholder's memory (as key positives or negatives). From memory comes belief and trust (or rejection), which in turn, leverages loyalty (or disloyalty) behavior.

If this seems in any way a linear process, be assured that it isn't. The many splendors of driving b2b or b2c customer, or employee, behavior are complex; but if the components are well understood and incorporated into strategic and tactical initiatives, these insights will help achieve desired marketplace or workplace actions.

And, just because an enterprise succeeds at reframing and redefining experiences (often through devices like journey mapping), they should also understand that sustaining perceived value and stakeholder commitment and loyalty is quite another matter. Reality, along with ever-changing stakeholder needs and tastes, dictates that the trust necessary to leverage decision making and behavior is extremely delicate and fragile. Once achieved, it needs to be guarded and protected. Again, like love.

Nowhere is trust more at constant risk than in financial services—banking, insurance, and investments. This stands to reason, since most consumers put great emotional and tangible return/coverage emphasis on protecting their earnings and nest eggs. Because this industry suffered such loss of trust during the recession, the companies that proactively show that they can create value and trust will be strategically differentiated, both in terms of culture and stakeholder value delivery. In TED-type fashion, there are several basic techniques for making this happen in the financial services industry:

1. Minimize irritating inefficiencies. For example, high-tech and virtual approaches may be great for the financial institution, but they often annoy and frustrate customers and put strain on employees.

2. Make the experience proactive and personal. Customers want to feel that interactions are personalized and that their needs are a priority. This also brings employees into closer proximity with customers, enhancing their commitment and job experience.

3. Practice transparent and frequent communication. A company can't go too far wrong if it assumes that the customer and employee want to be kept current on important transactional details (without having to ping the provider); and, at the same time, the customer wants the provider available to answer questions thoroughly and conveniently, another area where employee behavior is featured.

4. Emphasize simplicity. The financial services industry gets a fairly well-deserved rap for making many insurance, investment, and banking transactions and decisions too complex and time-consuming. The rule here should be, as MBNA used to preach (before being acquired by Bank of America): "Think of yourself as the customer." Customers will always lean toward simplicity because it feels more honest and open. And, again, this works on the employee side of the equation as well.

5. Understand your customers. Don't just find out what satisfies them. Find out what creates and undermines personal advocacy and bonding behavior, identify where experience can be improved. This "rule" applies, equally, to employees.

"If You Were the Only Girl in the World": Being Real with the Emotional Employee–Customer Connection

This sweet old song "If You Were the Only Girl in the World," with words by Clifford Grey and music by Nat Ayer, and written in 1916, has special meaning on Valentine's Day ... or any day. The song contains some lines, which have great employee ambassadorial metaphors, saying a lot about emotional connection and personalization between a vendor's employees and customers (Figure 6.2).

Here are a couple of fun examples, and questions to go with them:

- "If you were the only girl in the world and I was the only boy, nothing else would matter in the world today": As an employee, does the experience provided on behalf of my employer feel personalized and special to the customer?
- "I would say such wonderful things to you ... there would be such wonderful things to do": Beyond lip service, is there perceived rational and emotional value in what is provided to customers, that is, is there intentional, differentiated overdelivery?

In Chapter 4, we discussed how Jeanne Bliss, in her book *I Love You More Than My Dog*, examined how organizations can create more personal, intimate, lasting, and valued relationships between the enterprise and the customer, even becoming beloved. Employees are central to the opportunity this represents, augmented by the culture and stakeholder-centric processes. In other words, ambassadorship can build passion and partnership between key stakeholder groups, and between these groups and the supplier company.

Figure 6.2 Sheet music for "If You Were the Only Girl in the World"

Source: Internet.

The Container Store was an example of organizations doing this right, and well. By creating transparency with employees and building trust with customers, they have built an impactful, emotional connection between the employee experience and CX. As stated on The Container Store's website, there is definite, purposeful integration between the customer's value requirements, what employees provide, and the products and services the company offers:

> Wherever you look in the store, there's a cheerful employee who's ready to help solve everything from the tiniest of storage problems to the most intimidating organizational challenges. We want our

customers to receive unparalleled service, along with fresh ideas and a very interactive shopping experience.

Creating a differentiated experience is not just about any one thing. It's a complex mix of so many things. But the ultimate reward, the validation that the experience was successful is what we call getting the customer dance. It's everything about the customer experience that happens in the store and continues on after that customer gets home. Her heart rate goes up, up, up with every interaction with the brand. It's about what occurs when she takes the product home and actually lives with it. We want her to do a little dance every time she opens that closet door in the morning because it's so beautifully organized. So perfect for her. Frankly, she feels an emotional connection to her closet. The product—the solution—it transcends value for her.

This also speaks to the emotional importance of enterprise culture, referenced early in this chapter. In their *Harvard Business Review* article, Barsade and O'Neill identified companies like Southwest Airlines, Whole Foods Market, The Container Store, and Zappos as companies listing love and/or caring among their corporate values. But, they also recognized that few organizations recognized how much the emotional culture influenced employee behavior, in both positive and negative ways. They cited, for example, how Vail Resorts cultivates joy among employees and how this, in turn, helps create positive experiences for guests.

Finally, Barsade and O'Neill identified how the elimination of cultural toxicity and the focus on love—the degree of employee affection, caring, and compassion that employees feel, and convey between each other—influences both their experiences and the experiences of customers. This cultural element extends to how hiring should be done, and to the employee life cycle in general, which is covered in Chapter 9. Emotions, and an emotionally based culture, can be cultivated. This even extends to the basic, more functional components of the employee experience.

Are Experience Consistency and Reliability Emotional Drivers?

As stakeholder experience consultants who focus on the emotional elements of value delivery, we are often asked about the behavioral role of tangible, rational, and functional elements of value and experience.

These include the factors we typically associate with quality: completeness, timeliness, cost, functionality, accuracy, and so on. What we most often find in our client experience assignments is that there is almost invariably an emotional underpinning to these value components. These aren't the big "wow" elements of experience and value that seem to get a lot of attention, but when experiences are consistent, they help to create customer trust when delivered well and tend to undermine trust and value perception when there are issues, which may cause concern.

A bit more esoteric, but no less fundamental and important, are those elements of experience and value that we identify as gray areas between strictly emotional and strictly tangible. For employees, these include things like consistency and reliability of messages and also management approaches. For customers, these include product and service reliability and consistency, delivery of an experience, and value, per customer perceptions, that fall inside of emotional, sometimes subconscious, parameters the customer considers as acceptable. Reliability and consistency, delivered to a customer's expectations or better, build a "bank account" of positive memory and trust. One of the things most well understood about reliability and consistency within expectations is that when these delivery components fall outside of, that is, below, customer expectations, they often trigger emotional responses, which drive strong memories and downstream behavior.

Think about it. On the consumer side, many of us can remember expectations of experience at a restaurant, supermarket, hotel, rented auto, insurance company, department or discount store, and so on, that haven't been met. It's often the elements of consistency and reliability with the experience that are most dominant in our memories.

They actively contribute to emotion and downstream behavior. Poorly trained retail staff, dirty hotel rooms, hot food delivered cold—the

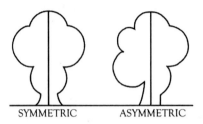

SYMMETRIC   ASYMMETRIC

Figure 6.3 Experience design consistency versus inconsistency

Source: Internet.

list goes on and on. In services, cable customers seem to get the most emotional on those rare occasions when their system goes down; and this can diminish confidence and trust in their supplier, sometimes enough to drive switching behavior. On the b2b customer side (Figure 6.3), it is things like consistent and reliable product quality, delivery timing, order completeness, service, and the like that contribute to memory.

As an example, a fast food distribution client once expressed disbelief that their 99.3 percent order completeness rate and 99.5 percent delivery timing rate did not drive higher customer loyalty. When their customers were interviewed, it was not the high order completeness and delivery timing rates that mattered, it was the emotion behind the memory of inconvenience and other problems caused by incomplete orders or delivery that was earlier or later than expected.

Because experience and value delivery are so often multichannel, even omnichannel, the consistency and reliability we're discussing must, today, extend across all modes of communication and conveyance. Customers expect experience reliability and consistency, irrespective of channel. This makes experience with these factors exponentially more impactful on customer behavior. When experience reliability suffers, consumer emotion and memory will trigger offline and word of mouth, usually negative.

The stats on this, and their behavioral impact, are well known. And then, irrespective of the channel, consumers' trust bank account will quickly be depleted; and, in the process, they will influence the bank accounts of other consumers. When consumers openly complain, telling others about lack of consistency and reliability and how it makes them feel, there is always the threat that this will "go viral."

Execs seem to focus more on what will drive the engaging, unexpected "wow" elements in experience and value delivery; however, it is well to remember that a strong structure is built on a solid foundation. Reliability and consistency, as much as other components of value, can strategically differentiate a business. Stephen Covey offers us some good guidelines for how to achieve this. In his Habit #7, Sharpen the Saw, he said, "The main thing is to keep the main thing the main thing." He also said, "Trust is the glue of life. It's the most essential ingredient in effective communication. It's the foundational principle that holds all relationships." This tells us a lot about the emotional power of consistency and reliability to all stakeholders. The reality, however, is that it has been most frequently neglected or superficially understood in employees.

CHAPTER 7

Measuring the Macro (Enterprise and Group) Level of Employee Ambassadorship

What Stakeholders Say Versus Mean Versus Do: Toward Understanding the Emotional and Subconscious Drivers of Behavior

Seemingly forever, marketers and researchers have been trying to identify stable and predictable links between what stakeholders, especially customers and employees, say about experiences, what they mean, that is, the emotional and unconscious underpinnings about what they really think and believe, and what they do in terms of actual decision making and actions in the marketplace and in their jobs.

There is an intersection between experience, internal reaction to that experience, informal peer-to-peer communication about the experience, and downstream customer decision making. It occurs in the personal emotional and subconscious distillation of that experience in forming the customer's behavior. This may sound a little technical and pop psychological for some, but reckoning with the meaning of emotional and subconscious response to experiences has important ramifications in the marketing world. It can mean knowing what customers *really* want. In the HR world, it can mean knowing what employees really want.

Some experiences are pleasurable in the subconscious, some are painful, some are superficial, some go deep. They can create sensations and feelings that can be a challenge to articulate but cause people to take action. Translating these subconscious emotions and feelings is the "holy grail" of customer and employee journey design.

As behavioral scientists report with frequency, workings of the subconscious mind, and understanding it, is the key to identifying the driving force behind actions. Learning, judgment, and a liberal amount of illogic and irrationality enters into the subconscious. Some actions take place as a result of the conscious, analytical and logical, but much of it comes from a deeper realm. Researchers in this field also tell us that, governed by the subconscious, humans can foresee and envision behavioral outcomes, and this is important to marketers.

My colleague Colin Shaw often points out that though Disney theme park vacationers and visitors often say they want salads and other healthy foods for themselves and their families, what they *really* want, and what they actually will buy, are hot dogs and hamburgers. If Disney only followed what customers said, they'd focus on salad; and this would diminish the overall park experience, potentially leading to churn. The same analogy can easily be applied to employees.

In another example, an IBM consumer study revealed that 43 percent of consumers said they preferred the "browse, click, and purchase experience," that is, shopping online and picking up in the store. However, only 29 percent reported using online shopping for their most recent store purchase. The reasons for this "say-do gap" have to do with trust and assurance issues—the need for on-demand customized promotions both online and in store, knowing beforehand that the desired product is in stock prior to making a trip to the store, ability to have personalized communication with a retailer when online, and so on. In other words, consumers want the digital experience to be seamless, irrespective of touch point or technology used. Understanding, and narrowing or eliminating, that say-mean-do gap gets us into the subconscious response to digital retail experiences.

Knowing what stakeholders really want, that is, what they mean when they say something, and how they will act and communicate to others, can be extremely impactful. Cracking the say-mean-do "code" enables marketers to interpret and translate the difference between consumer-stated comments, complaints, and concerns and how they can frequently translate in terms of actual behavior. Here are a few:

"Your product/service should be more like your competitor's" often really means they like your product/service but they prefer what the competitor offers.

"I think your product/service concept is great" often really means that a first impression, that is, the concept, is positive but may not lead to positive experience and action.

"I'd like to have this product/service feature" often really means that they likely have fundamental issues with a product or service, and that a better understanding of why customers want this feature, and/or would prefer an alternative.

"I regularly use your product/service" often really means that because memory is selective, they recall having used the product/service (at least once) in the past.

"I really like your product/service" really means that they don't love the product/service and that it needs to be improved.

"I'd pay more for this service" often really means that when push comes to shove, they wouldn't, believing that they deserve more value for the same price.

"I'd be glad to recommend your product/service" often really means that any such recommendation could range from bland and passive, or even negative, to active and enthusiastic.

Couldn't these same, or similar, questions be asked of employees? How well they respond will help identify their level of commitment and ambassadorship.

Stakeholder recommendation deserves special treatment in assessing results of the say-mean-do gap. Very often, claims of correlation between what customers say, mean, and do with respect to positive, neutral, or negative recommendation leaves out the actual causes, or levers, of emotional and unconscious processing.

As an example, in customer research, actionability of the one-number recommendation score question has been factually challenged by many practitioners, as have other elements of the research. Among multiple issues, the question asks, "Would you recommend …" rather than "Will you recommend …" or "Have you recommended …"

The latter two variations are considered superior since, in the case of the first variation, the question calls for customers to have greater emotional and subconscious certainty; and, in the case of the second variation, there is real evidence of having taken action, that is, actually behaved. The same thesis, incidentally, applies to employee recommendation.

For employees, recommendation simply isn't enough to identify level of ambassadorship.

There are many more problems with putting too much emphasis on stated potential recommendation and referral, and taking them as direct surrogates for actual meaning and intended or real action. One of these problems is that if other information is available about customer (or employee) behavior, as it often is through targeted emotional driver research, the overfocus on a single number suggests that these more in-depth insights will receive less consideration and relevance. For example, if a company discovers that it has a high incidence of unaddressed and/or unresolved stakeholder complaints, a situation certainly jammed with emotional and subconscious feelings, that serious loyalty-leveraging situation can get low priority, and might even be brushed aside, as executives seek to create ever-higher positive recommendation levels.

Again, knowing what stakeholders really want in their experiences and what they'll really do, often despite what they say they'd do, can be critical to a business. So as my British friends would say, "Mind the gap." What they mean is "Be careful not to get your foot caught in the open space. It'll hurt."

MROC 'n Roll: Generating Social Connectivity and Valuable Insights from Employee and Customer Communities

Over the past few years, we have seen the growth of b2b and b2c market research online communities, or MROCs. Companies can, for example, conduct qualitative research, such as juries and panels to evaluate alternative communication concepts and executions.

They can do straight customer loyalty and customer value research by recruiting panels of forum participants. Typically, these surveys are conducted on an intranet basis. Results are immediate, and companies using their forum participants as panelists get response rates high enough to avoid the nonresponse bias pitfalls of other, lower-response, self-completion research methods. Further, companies using their communities for value and experience research can link results to projected, segmented customer profitability, a tremendous benefit.

In what Harley Manning and Kerry Bodine call the "Customer Experience Ecosystem," engaging employees who are both visible to customers and those behind the scenes (i.e., all employees) can directly impact the customer journey and customer experience (CX) initiatives. Tapping internal knowledge and expertise through "voice of the employee" (VoE) programs has seen increased acceptance in recent years. Through such programs, employees can offer ideas for improving CX, cocreate, offer perspectives on the ideas of others, and help track these ideas from the first spark to final implementation.

Communication with employees, and, for example, the way employee evaluations are communicated can enhance both the individual's job experience and the impact on customer behavior. Amazon, a leader in CX is also trailblazing in the manner in which employee reviews are fed back. Per an Amazon spokesperson: "We're launching a new annual review process next year (2017) that is radically simplified on our employees' strengths, not the absence of weaknesses." This type of positive employee reinforcement directly influences how they interact with customers. Temkin Group research has identified that 85 percent of employees who receive positive performance feedback from management completely agree that they would recommend their employers' products and services.

This is just a taste of where positive communication, between employees and between employees and customers, can lead. Innovative, positive, social techniques are core to employee voice of the customer (VoC) (aka VoE) programs. Just as captive customer MROCs can provide excellent customer-related information, much the same can be said for employee MROCs. Very often, this is a partnership between marketing and HR. Though at present, these communities are far less prevalent, employee MROCs represent tremendous, cost-effective learning and insight potential.

Almost identical to consumer and customer MROCs, employee market research communities offer every enterprise the opportunity to:

- Create a dialogue—Employees can offer their perspectives in a nonthreatening, secure environment. Most MROCs provide the option to sign up anonymously, and interact with the online community manager. In addition, company stakeholders can listen in, or review transcripts, to go deeper into employee and employee–customer issues, with breaking continuity.

- Generate cross enterprise insights—Building from the perspective that every employee has roles and responsibilities in delivering value and optimizing CX, organizations can provide actionable, objective bottom-up information. In addition, ideas can be tested on this basis.

- Have tremendous flexibility—Employee communities, and research subject panels, can be run for set periods of time or on an open-ended basis. This gives the organization and the employees a great deal of contribution flexibility. Depending on what the organization needs, community research participation by employees can be open-ended or have fixed end dates.

One of the greatest benefits of employee MROCs is that the processes and mechanics of these communities enables employees to be more empowered, to feel that they are heard, and that they are helping guide in decisions important to the organization. At the same time, employee communities are social entities for their corporate sponsors, enabling companies to build relationships and provide more fulfilling and engaging experiences.

An excellent example of an organization that drives customer and employee advocacy through social engagement is TD Bank. Wendy Arnott, TD Bank's VP of Social Media and Digital Marketing, has built a social media program from the inside out. For several years, TD Bank has been able to connect employees across business segments and geographies, as well as leverage employee knowledge, build communities of interest, recognize and collaborate, and ultimately deliver business values. As she has stated, "We wanted to give a voice to our employees and open up two-way conversation." In an industry like banking, often considered a business of inches played over years, this is both great for employee experience optimization and competitive differentiation.

Employee Ambassadorship Research: Where (and Why) We Began, Where We Are, Where We're Going

During his 50-year career, John Wayne made over 170 movies. Arguably, one of the worst was *The Barbarian and the Geisha*, released in 1958, in which he played Townsend Harris, the United States' first official envoy to Japan. The movie wasn't particularly memorable (although the scenery was beautiful), but the movie makes a critical point about the concept of ambassadorship. Harris' specific assignment, through words and actions, was to create trust among the Japanese nobility as a foundation for full diplomatic relations. Because, at the time the movie took place (1856), Japan regarded the motives of every foreign country with fear and mistrust, establishing and maintaining a stable, positive relationship was a formidable task.

What is important here is that this story is not at all dissimilar to the relationship every company has, and would like, with each customer, particularly through the attitudes and behaviors of employees. Companies have, increasingly, worked to align the enterprise around the customer's needs, value delivery, and make the organization more customer centric. Trust and value provision are the dual goals of all customer–supplier interactions; and, because employees are so central in creating and/or maintaining trust, their role in the linkage of value delivery to customer behavior must be better understood. This is accomplished through a leading-edge new approach to employee research, with the central theses of creating stronger emotional connection and executing ambassadorial behavior.

An ambassador, according to the dictionary, is an official or unofficial diplomat, the representative of a country or an organization. As applied to employee research, we view ambassadorship as having direct connection to the concept of customer advocacy, that is, the active expression of commitment. Employee ambassadors, then, represent the highest level of commitment (or the lowest level, which we identify as "sabotage") to the company's product or service value promise, to the organization itself, and to the customers. The contribution of employees is incredibly

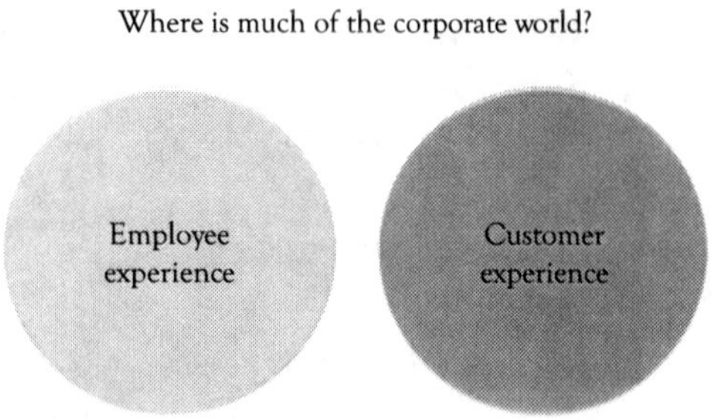

Where is much of the corporate world?

Figure 7.1 Silos of employee and customer experience

Source: Beyond Philosophy (www.beyondphilosophy.com).

pivotal to organizational success and survival, particularly as it pertains to customers.

The challenge, however, is that much of the corporate world does not look to link, align, and integrate the employee experience into a dynamic. Most organizations, in fact, silo the employee experience and CX (Figure 7.1).

First, Some Employee Research Landscape Definitions

Most HR managers and executives, indeed most managers and executives in almost every company, are familiar with the terms *employee satisfaction* and *employee engagement*. We've discussed these in previous chapters, so for purposes of building on this foundation, we're repeating them here. Not so familiar, though, is employee commitment, which is where the learning and insight opportunity, and the connection between employee experience and CX, resides.

> *Employee Satisfaction and Loyalty Research*—Identifies attitudes and behaviors leading to job satisfaction and loyalty to company. This is very traditional employee research, which has been around for generations.
>
> *Employee Engagement and Alignment Research*—Identifies attitudes and actions leading to agreement with, and belief in, overall company mission/objectives, as well as degree of perceived "fit" within

organizational culture. This is employee research, which has gained acceptance and application by HR professionals and consultants over the past 10 to 15 years.

Paraphrasing TQ guru W. Edwards Deming, everyone in the organization must understand his/her role in customer relationships, and this should be evident to the customer as well. To optimize the employee experience and CX, organizations need to define the experience they are trying to deliver for both stakeholder groups and the role emotions and memory play. Building on that platform, companies need to determine which experience components drive the most value. This, then, will lead to identifying how they design deliberate, positive, and memorable customer and employee experiences. The employee research challenge, however, is that neither employee satisfaction/loyalty nor employee engagement/alignment research have been able to do this very consistently or well.

There is growing recognition of the need for a third employee research approach, one that relates and links employee emotions, perceptions, and actions to key company business and financial missions and strategies, particularly regarding customer behaviors on behalf of the employer. As noted, very little employee research (qualitative or quantitative) has been conducted, and no proven technique had been created, in these areas. As noted, we call the concept forming the research method we have developed *employee ambassadorship*. This represents the more contemporary, and more actionable, reality of optimizing employee productivity, connecting to the organization, and focusing on delivering value to customers; and it addresses the direct and indirect behavioral linkages between these stakeholder groups.

So, the three "branches" of employee research, now incorporating the new branch of employee ambassadorship, can be illustrated as follows (Figure 7.2).

As customer research has evolved over the past 30 years, to now have more of a focus on the rational and emotional components of value, so too has employee research begun to become more contemporary and real world. Employee satisfaction and engagement research are indeed useful foundational techniques, but they are far less effective at going beyond intuitive assumptions regarding employees' specific impact on,

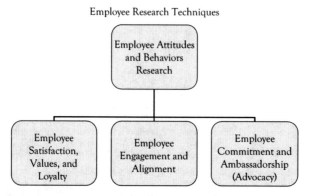

Employee Research Techniques

Figure 7.2 Employee research technique branches

Source: Author.

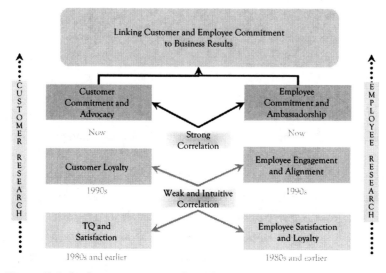

Figure 7.3 Linking customer and employee commitment to business results; TQ, total quality

Source: Author.

and linkage to, customer behavior. We have illustrated this evolution in the following graphic (Figure 7.3).

As discussed, unlike employee engagement, which has been around since the 1990s, ambassadorship is a fairly ahead-of-the-curve term and represents an updated set of approaches in understanding employee and customer behavior, and there has not been a great deal of academic literature on it (and none from professional employee research sources); but it's quickly becoming more actively used. Simply stated, ambassadorship involves both the employee's level of emotional affinity/kinship, action-based state of relationship with a brand or supplier, plus the positive and negative ways/messages they communicate to others about their employer's brands and suppliers.

In other words, ambassadorship is the active and vocal expression of commitment or bonding to the organization on the positive side, and disconnection or sabotage, active undermining of the company, when there is negative commitment. Employee attitudes and beliefs can result in these kinds of polar behaviors, defined as follows.

Employee Ambassadors (Advocates)—the most active level, representing employees who are strongly committed to the company's product and service promise, the organization itself, and its customers. Also, and importantly, they behave and communicate in a consistently positive manner toward the company, both inside and outside.

Employee Saboteurs—employees who, though still drawing a paycheck from the company, are active, and frequently vocal, detractors about the organization itself, its culture and policies, and its products and services. These individuals are negative advocates, communicating their low opinions and unfavorable perspectives both to peers inside the company and to customers, and others, outside the company.

Companies are fond of saying that employees are their most powerful resource, and in many ways—especially their influence on customer loyalty behavior—that's been well proven. But, to understand what factors leverage employee behavior, most organizations have historically relied on satisfaction and engagement surveys, typically conducted through HR. However, there is little realization that these traditional research techniques are not remotely designed to identify the often hidden factors behind this behavior. This is particularly true when endeavoring to identify employees' level of commitment to the company, to its product and/or service value proposition, and to its customers.

In building our basic employee ambassadorship framework, we begin where many HR professionals and consultants start, with the core components of employee engagement, based on fit, alignment, and productivity. We have stated these earlier in the book, but they are worth repeating here:

- *Commitment to Company*—Commitment to, and being positive about, the company (through personal satisfaction and an expression of pride), and to being a contributing, and fully aligned, *member of the culture*
- *Commitment to Value Proposition*—Commitment to, and alignment with, the mission and goals of the company, as expressed through perceived excellence (benefits and solutions) provided by products and/or services

So, employees that score high on commitment to the company and the value proposition are, from this characterization, considered engaged. This is a starting point. Moving to holistic employee focus, commitment, and ambassadorship, with a strong emphasis on the employee experience, we add in customer commitment:

- *Commitment to Customers and Value Delivery*—Commitment to understanding customer needs, and to performing in a manner that provides customers with optimal emotional experiences, memories, and relationships, as well as delivering the highest level of product and/or service value

Again, as shown earlier in the book (but repeated here for emphasis), ambassadorship can be graphically expressed as follows (Figure 7.4).

As early ambassadorship research clearly identified, in comparison to engagement and satisfaction approaches, this is an enhanced method for creating, adjusting, or sustaining employee commitment to drive downstream customer loyalty behavior. The key, it has been determined, is to focus on developing and supporting employees, and providing a more fulfilling experience, so that they, in turn create unique value-add CXs. Again, optimizing CX is, or should be, part of every employee's job description.

Macro, that is, industrywide and general demographic, employee ambassadorship research (conducted through The Harris Poll several

Employees That Score High on Commitment to the Company, The Value
Proposition, and the Customer Are Considered Ambassadors

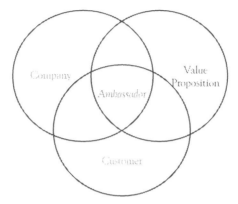

Figure 7.4 Employee ambassadorship research framework

Source: Author.

years ago) told us a great deal about what was forming, or detracting
from, this behavior, especially where measurement of commitment to
customers and value delivery were concerned. Here are some results from
our key ambassadorship indicator questions:

1. *Do you tell others how bad the products or services of the company you
   work for are?*
   Overall: Yes, frequently (3%), Yes, sometimes (32%), Net (35%);
   No, never (65%)

   This was higher in the East, and among black respondents (41%);
   lower among respondents 50 to 64 years (28%) and those over 65
   years (25%), but higher among 18- to 24-year-olds (42%). Males
   are also more negative about their company's products and services
   than are females (39% vs. 30%). Those who identified their sexual
   orientation as LGBT also were significantly more negative (60%).
   There was also marked impact of polarity by income level: Forty-four
   percent of respondents with $34,900, or less, compared to 31% with
   $75,000+. Finally, there was more tendency to tell consumers nega-
   tive things (compared to businesses) and to speak negatively about
   products compared to services.

2. *Do you tell others how good the products or services of the company you work for are?*

Overall: Yes, frequently (38%), Yes, sometimes (50%), Net (88%); No, never (12%)

As a quick observation, there was a marked proclivity of employees to be positive *and* vocal about their employer's products and/or services, compared to the likelihood of being negative *and* vocal. Nevertheless, the impact on customer behavior of both needs to be understood—which is the value of both mirroring and ambassadorship research.

Interestingly, younger employees were much more likely to be positive about products and services compared to employees over 65 years (91% to 80%). When we asked employees to say why they believed their company does not earn customer trust and loyalty, here is what we learned:

- Profit is the only motivation for company (11%)—Told more to consumers (than to businesses)
- Poor customer service (11%)—Told more to consumers (than to businesses)
- Lie to customers (10%)—Almost entirely by Baby Boomers, also more frequently from those with H.S. or less education; told more about products than services
- Inconsistent policies/treat different customers differently (9%)—Strongly from Baby Boomers, also more frequently from those with H.S. or less education; told more about products than services
- Do not treat employees fairly (9%)—Strongly from Baby Boomers, also more frequently from those with H.S. or less education; told more about products than services

3. *Do you tell others how bad your company is as a place to work?*

Overall: Yes, frequently (7%), Yes, sometimes (35%), Net (43%); No, never (57%)

Lower frequency of this was in the South. There was greater frequency among Echo Boomers (49%), significantly lower percentages among Matures, 62+ years (25%). Higher among males than females. Lower among blacks. Higher among those with low-est income (48%), and lower among highest income respondents (37%). Very high among respondents with disabilities (52%) com-pared to those with no disabilities (40%). Finally, more negatives about companies making products (48%).

4. *Do you tell others how good your company is as a place to work?*
   Overall: Yes, frequently (34%), Yes, sometimes (48%), Net (82%); No, never (18%)

   Lowest frequent personal positive communication was by 18- to 24-year-olds (24%), highest among the 65+ age group (43%). Also, it was somewhat higher among those with postgraduate degree and those with higher income.

Ambassadorship is linked to the productivity and empowerment ele-ments of employee satisfaction, engagement, and alignment research; however, through this early research we learned that it is more closely correlated with, and directly helps drive, business results and value build-ing because its emphasis is building customer bonds through direct and indirect employee interaction.

This original ambassadorship approach was developed and tested during 2006. The framework proved very successful for clients in multi-ple industries; and they have found the results both insightful and highly useful in prioritizing their employee training and communication around the customer. More recently, a team of loyalty and stakeholder research consultants and methodologists conducted exhaustive qualitative and quantitative new baseline research to further refine the ambassadorship technique and make it even more contemporary and actionable for clients.

Early in 2008, we conducted second-generation employee research through the Harris Poll, among 4,300 adults who are employed full-time. Sample size was sufficient to provide baseline results in close to 20 major business and industry areas.

The questionnaire utilized for this study was constructed based on both the earlier ambassadorship research protocol and insights from the qualitative research. The "three legs" of the ambassadorship research stool, identified earlier, consisted of nine dependent attributes, or agree/disagree scale statements (three in each of the legs). In addition, a number of loyalty and advocacy (positive and negative communication) metrics were used to help validate the new ambassadorship framework.

As in the original research, we most typically concentrated on what drives active, positive, vocal employee commitment, that is, ambassadorship; however, it was at least equally important to identify where employee indifference and negativism, potentially leading to sabotage attitudes and actions, exist, why they exist, and how they can be mitigated or eliminated. Again stating what we have come to learn: If employee ambassadorship is the North Pole, then sabotage is the South Pole.

Overall Employee Ambassadorship Second-Generation Baseline Study Results

Similar to the original employee ambassadorship research conducted in 2006, the updated 2008 study showed that about 15.5 percent of adults, employed full-time and working for a company, were identified through the framework as ambassadors. At the opposite end of the commitment spectrum, those employees we identify through framework scoring as saboteurs, about 29.5 percent qualified to be in this group. This was significantly higher than the 10 percent of employees tagged as saboteurs in the original, first-generation round of ambassadorship research.

Several industry groups had ambassadorship and sabotage levels at approximately the same percentages as overall full-time employees:

- Education
- Healthcare and Social Assistance
- Technology Services
- Banking and Finance
- Engineering Services
- Insurance

There were, as well, industry groups with very high ambassadorship levels, coupled with low sabotage levels: Religious and Nonprofit organizations, Construction, and Legal Services. Conversely, there were several industry groups with very low ambassadorship and high sabotage levels: Telecommunications, Retail Trade, Manufacturing, Transportation and Warehousing, and Accommodation and Food Services. It's interesting to note that, especially in telecom, retailing, lodging and food services, these are some of the industries so often featured in business studies and trade stories and articles as representing the poorest reported CXs and highest levels of service complaint.

Second-Generation Ambassadorship Research Key Findings

In addition to employee motivation, cohesion, productivity, and alignment with corporate values and culture, HR is perhaps most interested and focused on learning how to increase staff loyalty, or at least their retention within the enterprise. Our research identified employee loyalty level through three specific metrics: rating of the organization as a place to work, likelihood to recommend the organization to friends or family members as a place to work, and level of felt, that is, emotional connection, loyalty to the organization. Overall, 18 percent of our respondents exhibited high loyalty to their organizations, and 20 percent exhibited low loyalty; and, importantly, there were also strong, almost polar opposite differences in organizational loyalty depending on whether an employee was categorized as an ambassador or saboteur:

Employee Loyalty* by Ambassador Group		
	Total	*Ambassador*	*Saboteur*
Low	19.8%	0.0%	61.0%
Medium	61.9%	27.3%	38.5%
High	18.3%	72.7%	0.5%
Total	100.0%	100.0%	100.0%

* Partial Least Squares (PLS) factor of the three metrics used to calculate employee loyalty.

These are definite "pay attention" findings for HR. It's a concern, of course, that almost 20 percent of employees have low organizational loyalty; however, it's an even greater challenge that there is three times the level of potential staff turnover among saboteurs, who, before they depart, will undermine the performance and loyalty of other employees. Our research provides very specific insights into why this is occurring. At the same time, the organization will be very well served to emulate the behaviors and attitudes of ambassadors through the rest of the culture.

Commitment to the company, in the form of loyalty and related attitudes and behaviors, is a fairly basic requirement for employee ambassadorship. As important is feeling that the company is both a good place to work and that its products and services are good, and communicating this belief to others, including colleagues, friends, and customers.

Similar to overall employee loyalty findings, ambassadors were found to be both positive and vocal promoters and representatives of the company as a place to work, while most saboteurs never, or less frequently, said anything good about the company as an employer. In terms of the highest frequency of saying positive things about the company as a place to be employed, ambassadors were over 40 times more likely to do this than saboteurs (85.7% compared to 2.1%).

Frequency of Saying Company Is a Good Place to Be Employed			
	Total	Ambassador	Saboteur
Rarely/never	20.4%	0.9%	55.5%
Sometimes/often	49.6%	13.4%	42.4%
Almost always/always	30.0%	85.7%	2.1%
Total	100.0%	100.0%	100.0%

When asked if they ever say anything bad about the company as a place to work, almost none of the ambassadors (1.9 percent) were frequent or occasional negative communicators in this regard. However, saboteurs were 26 times more likely to communicate to others in negative ways, either frequently or occasionally (49.4 percent). It's clear that this kind of attitude and behavior can have significant impact on attracting the best employees, keeping them, and having them be focused on customers.

The third principal component of ambassadorship is representing the company's products and services, that is, its brand promise to others, both inside and outside of the organization. Similar to their responses regarding the company as a place of employment, the disparity in saying good things about the company's products and services between ambassadors and saboteurs was dramatic: Over 20 times more ambassadors always or almost always said positive things compared to saboteurs (78.3% vs. 3.7%).

Frequency of Saying Company's Products/Services Are Good			
	Total	Ambassador	Saboteur
Rarely/never	18.1%	1.6%	45.0%
Sometimes/often	54.1%	20.1%	50.3%
Almost always/always	27.8%	78.3%	3.7%
Total	100.0%	100.0%	100.0%

Interestingly, the 78 percent of ambassadors frequently saying that the company's products and services are good (in our 2008 research) was not very different than the 85 percent of the employees making product and service recommendations after receiving positive performance feedback from management (in Temkin Group's 2016 research, cited earlier in this chapter). Saying negative things about the company's products or services was also significantly more prevalent among saboteurs. Over 45 percent of employee saboteurs said negative things about products or services at least some of the time, compared to only 2.6 percent of ambassadors.

What we learned from this early ambassadorship research is that companies should evaluate the effectiveness of rules and metrics associated with delivering customer value. For instance, how effective is the company, and employees, at unearthing and resolving unexpressed complaints, which may be undermining customer loyalty? How are nonfinancial metrics viewed relative to financial ones? What types of automated support processes exist, and how well are employees trained in them, to make serving customers easier? How does the company balance taking care of existing customers, particularly those who may be at risk of defection, with acquiring new ones? How much cross functional collaboration exists in support of the customer?

For companies to create and sustain higher levels of employee ambassadorship, it's necessary to have customer and employee intelligence specifically designed to close gaps between CX, outmoded internal beliefs, and rudimentary support and training. It's also essential that the *employee experience* be given as much emphasis as CX. If ambassadorship is to flourish, there must be value, and a sense of shared purpose, for the employee as well as the company and customer—in the form of recognition, reward (financial and training), and career opportunities.

Everybody Wins: Focus on Your Employees *Because* of Your Customers

When moving to the third generation of employee ambassadorship research, we looked at the following key issues. Everyone knows the classic questions regarding evolution: Which came first, cowboys or saloons? Chickens or eggs? While these may be ongoing issues in cultural anthropology or biology, the role of employees in leveraging CX and loyalty behavior is far simpler to understand. Along with powerful, detailed data and a customer-centric culture, it's impossible to have customer commitment and advocacy behavior without employees both understanding their role as CX stakeholders and living that role as value delivery agents and company ambassadors.

As discussed throughout the book, it has been found that employee commitment and advocacy behavior—on behalf of the company's product and service value proposition, the organization itself, and the customers—has a direct and profound relationship, or linkage, to the behavior of customers and also to corporate sales and profitability. As extensive academic and professional research into this effect concludes with regularity, employee attitudes and actions, especially around customer commitment and customer transactional experiences, and championing a company's products or services can't be separated from the effective delivery of customer value.

Yet, when considering, and measuring, the pivotal elements of staff performance and productivity, most companies are focused principally on employee attitudes around satisfaction, company loyalty, alignment with goals and objectives (such as corporate citizenship), and levels of engagement. These are important, to be sure but, historically, they only superficially and incidentally correlate to what employees think and do to customer behavior.

Critically, employee engagement research, in its most frequently executed forms, often misses what actually drives positive employee experience and how that connects to CX. Sir Richard Branson has been quoted as saying: "If you take care of your people, they'll take care of your businesses." The reality, however, is not quite that simple and straightforward. More actionable insights need to be gathered, which address factors that define and support the linkage between the employee experience and CX optimization, so that there is real value for both of these key stakeholder groups.

We have developed a third-generation research framework for identifying what creates, or detracts from, employee commitment behavior, which we call ambassadorship. Its intent is to identify the most active level of employee belief in, and actions on behalf of, the company's product and service value promise, to the company itself, and to optimizing CX. It is linked to, but distinctive from, the productivity and empowerment elements of employee satisfaction, engagement, and alignment research. However, here the emphasis is on strengthening bonds with customers, creating positive transactional and long-term CX through employee interaction, and building a more fulfilling employee experience.

Employees actions, including expressing themselves face-to-face and through digital means, directly and indirectly impact much of what we understand about CX emotion and memory, leading to downstream behavior. So there are challenges, but also rewards, with generating insights about employee emotions and what actually creates experience value.

Our employee research includes multiple categories of attributes, many of which would be found, in one form or another, in engagement studies: Cohesion, Satisfaction, Business Alignment, Career and Growth, Management Effectiveness, and Morale and Culture. What employee engagement studies don't include, however, is Customer Focus as a key attribute category, with diagnostics such as:

- The functions I perform contribute to the company's delivery of customer value.
- Cross-training enables me to provide better value to customers.
- The company is customer focused.
- I understand customers' value priorities.
- Management listens to my ideas on creating value for customers.
- The company has a clearly defined mission for creating customer value.
- New products and services for customers are clearly communicated within the company.
- I have the tools and resources I need to provide value to customers.

This is just a small sample. In our research, we typically include between 20 and 25 Customer Focus attributes, out of about 40 total. Through sophisticated analysis, what they reveal speaks volumes about the degree of cross enterprise customer centricity by various groups within a company, and also the level of stakeholder centricity inherent in the culture.

Third-Generation Technique: Bringing Employee Ambassadorship Research Up-To-Date and Making It Even More Real World and Actionable

One of our initial third-generation ambassadorship projects was pathfinding employee behavior research for a major insurance company. Uniquely, the focus of this research was on emotional and subconscious value drivers, and it represents the third, and most contemporary and actionable, generation of employee ambassadorship research. After working with a cross-sectional team of client supervisors and managers, we jointly identified a total of nine employee attribute and touch point groupings, and a total of 40 individual elements. Several factors made this research process particularly distinctive:

- As noted in the description of our research technique from the previous section, almost half of the attributes had to do with employee/group customer focus and degree of business alignment, rarely, if ever, addressed in employee studies. We also addressed leadership, advancement, training, work environment, bonding, availability of tools, and teamwork.
- We incorporated multiple value indicators in the research, that is, accepted drivers of employee job satisfaction (including loyalty) and engagement (personal commitment to the success of the organization and strength of personal belief in the goals and objectives of the organization), which are often seen in these studies. Included among the new set of employee experience value drivers were commitment/ambassadorship (frequency of telling others how good or bad they think the company's products and/or services are, and strength of belief

that the company's products and/or services exceed customer expectations), which are almost never addressed.

- The protocol also included components that looked at the emotional (and usually unexplored) responses of employees regarding their job experience, that is, how they feel, such as the level of trust, stress, frustration, and so on. (Note: The full spectrum and behavioral influence of these emotions is expressed in the Foreword Figure F.1.)

Our third-generation method yielded many useful and actionable insights, including overall effect, the experience value outcomes that the organization produces from employee behavior. Again, this is very different than what can be learned from employee satisfaction and engagement research.

From the research for our insurance client, there were a number of powerful results, many of which they had never seen from HR-led employee engagement studies. For example, while there were positive results in the categories of business alignment and customer focus, this was counterbalanced by challenges in areas of advancement (career opportunity, salary, responsiveness to employee needs and suggestions, etc.) and bonding (use of feedback for improvement, involvement in decisions that affect the employee's work, etc.).

Other value-deflating or impairing elements for employees included response to training and cross-training, the level of trust in/approachability of management, freedom to express ideas, feeling that their contribution as team members was appreciated, and a belief among the surveyed employees that their department had greater focus on customers than other groups within the organization.

Further, when our emotional profile was layered onto the results, employees' feelings of frustration and stress (especially among those more tenured), and feeling hurried in their work requirements, had the potential of seriously impairing both employee behavior and CX. Also, longer-tenured employees showed lower positive emotional ratings, often at a significant level when compared to newer employees.

Our assessment of what positively enhanced and negatively inhibited employee value delivery, on both a conscious and subconscious level, showed that it was clearly the subconscious and memorable aspects of employee experience that drove most organizational value.

Again, supported by reaction from HR management when results were presented, our employee ambassadorship study findings produced results quite unlike their prior research that had been built around a satisfaction or engagement approach:

- Because of teamwork and shared information issue challenges identified, degree of enterprise customer centricity was called into question.
- Tenure emerged as a pivotal employee issue. On entering the client's building, we saw the following sign posted in their front hall (which helped confirm this finding) (Figure 7.5).
- Customer Focus and Business Alignment emerged as very important elements of experience in understanding employee value and must be added to future employee surveys.
- Challenges in employee career advancement and bonding must be addressed.

Figure 7.5 Main hallway sign welcoming new hires at client office

Source: Beyond Philosophy (www.beyondphilosophy.com).

The tenure aspects of what we learned deserve a bit more space here, because they were both important and, as other elements discussed in the preceding text, previously unknown or minimally addressed by HR from their earlier employee satisfaction and engagement studies. Here are just some of the highlights:

- Though loyalty to the company remained high as tenure increased, personal belief in the company's goals and objectives and belief that the company's products and services exceed customer expectations declined as length of employment went beyond 5 and 10 years.
- All of the Leadership attributes, and many of the Customer Focus and Business Alignment attributes declined over length of employment, reaching the lowest level after 10 years as an employee. In addition, there was decline in Training, Advancement (salary, career, changing employee needs, promotion selection process), Environment, and Team attribute categories.
- Job satisfaction showed significant decline with increased tenure.
- The most significant tenure-related declines were in "Selection process for promotions is fair and consistent" and "I have involvement in decisions that affect my work."

Our Emotional Profile, examining levels of all 20 emotions each client employee in the study was asked to assess from a personal job experience standpoint (again, see Foreword [Figure F.1]), clearly showed that after a "romancing" period of the first 11 months, employees feel less positive and significantly more stressed, dissatisfied, and disappointed. Though declines were seen after 10 years of employment, the greatest levels of entropy (fall-off of positive emotions, increase of negative emotions, and defined by Merriam-Webster as "a process of degradation or running down or a trend to disorder") were seen at between 1 and 5 years of tenure.

In fact, after 1 year of employment, all of the positive emotions were lower and the negative emotions were higher on a statistically significant basis and remained so after 10 years as an employee (see Figure 7.6).

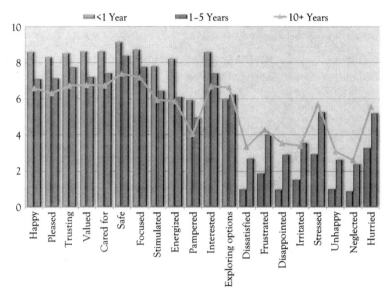

Figure 7.6 Employee emotional profile at under 1 year, 1 to 5 years, and over 10 years of tenure

Source: Beyond Philosophy (www.beyondphilosophy.com).

So, we concluded that (a) the subconscious and memorable aspects of the employee experience drove the most value, and (b) emotional and other tenure-related perceptual issues were going to be pivotal going forward if our client was to launch initiatives to create greater ambassadorship among its employees.

As noted, W. Edwards Deming always counseled organizations that all employees have one of two jobs within the enterprise: They either directly support the customer or support someone who does. This is the essence of employee ambassadorship. Though I've conducted a great deal of earlier-generation employee ambassadorship research over the past decade, application of the emotionally based protocol for this purpose was a very positive and productive learning experience, a foundation for further development. As noted earlier, there were valuable and prioritized insights for our client, the service component of the insurance company, to leverage going forward, and significant implications for the broader organization as well.

Employee commitment and advocacy, that is, ambassadorship, has begun to be a major goal of many organizations, as they have come to realize the financial and cultural consequences of a workforce that is cohesive, focused, committed, and productive around the overarching mission of optimizing customer loyalty and advocacy behavior.

CHAPTER 8

Addressing and Assessing the Impact of Employee Negativism and How a Stakeholder-Centric Culture Can Fix This

A recent *Wall Street Journal* "At Work" column led with this sentence: "U.S. employers have a trust problem." According to a newly released report on work and employee well-being research conducted by the American Psychological Association (APA):

- Only about half of U.S. workers feel their employers are up-front with them.
- One-quarter of American workers simply don't trust their employers.

That's not good news for business, and it's not good news for customers.

Companies display their humanity, stakeholder centricity, and cultural investment in a number of key ways, two of which are employee compensation and, perhaps more important, opportunity for professional growth, contribution, and advancement. In the APA study, conducted among over 1,500 working adults, under half of the employees felt that they are sharing in the gains realized by their employers as they recover from the deep 2008 recession. This is, as reflected in the statistics in the preceding text, a disturbing finding because of the impact it has on employee commitment to the company, to the company's product and service value proposition, and to the company's customers (Figure 8.1).

Figure 8.1 Negative or apathetic employee

Source: Internet.

It has been well documented that today's empowered customers are demanding more from brands—convenience, anticipatory service, and (ideally) real-time and contextual personalization, at all points of interaction, which some call omnichannel.

However the experience is viewed, in most of the touch point situations, employees are directly or indirectly involved (and, if not, they should be). It's vital that they be positive and supportive of the brand value proposition, and the organization itself, as well as the customers—in other words, to be ambassadors. Trust and commitment are central, and basic, to driving employee ambassadorship, and every enterprise must understand where trust and commitment, as cultural elements, are practiced well and where low levels of it can impact both employee and customer behavior.

For companies to create and sustain higher levels of employee ambassadorship, it's necessary to have customer and employee intelligence specifically designed to close the gaps caused by commoditized, passive customer experience (CX), outmoded internal beliefs, poor hiring practices, and rudimentary support and training. It's also essential that the *employee experience* be given as much emphasis as CX.

If ambassadorship is to flourish, there must be value, and a sense of involvement and shared purpose, for the employee as well as the company and customer—in the form of job performance recognition, reward (financial and training), and career opportunities.

Comparing Perceived Value Drivers for Employees and Customers

Some may remember an episode of the 90s sitcom *Murphy Brown* in which Candace Bergen, as Murphy, was viewing a focus group about her news program, *FYI*, in the client room through the two-way mirror. In a key scene, focus group participants were asked to describe the personalities, investigative technique impressions, and overall presentation styles of various team members of the program—beginning with Corky, Frank, and Jim; and they did so in positive, glowing terms. When they got to descriptions of Murphy, however, the perceptions turned to sharply negative. Murphy was roundly identified as abrasive, abrupt, and insensitive, just a few of the unflattering characterizations of her interviewing and reporting style on the program as considered by this group of viewers.

Hearing and seeing this, Murphy jumped from her chair, charged out of the client viewing room and emotionally confronted the focus group members, asserting that, deep down, she is really warm and caring, and questioning—pleading, really—why viewers didn't see her in that light. Though played for laughs, this scene was all too representative of the value delivery perceptual gaps, which often have been found to exist between suppliers and their customers. The reality, learned from many studies, is that employees frequently see both the importance and the performance of key rational and emotional value drivers very differently when compared to customers.

Years ago, as discussed earlier, quality guru W. Edwards Deming said that what everyone in a company does can be reduced to one of two functions: (a) to serve the customer or (b) serve someone who does. So, arguably, understanding where perceptual gaps between employees and customers exist anywhere in the company should be of prime importance to HRD, especially in their capacity of helping optimize the effectiveness of human resources. The reality is that all levels of management should share in this.

In preparation for *Customer WinBack*, my 2001 book on customer loss and recovery coauthored with Jill Griffin, we conducted original research among purchasing agents and sales/marketing managers to better understand the essential value delivery perceptual differences between customers and suppliers. This was what we called "mirroring" or obtaining a reflection.

Our sample included a statistically valid cross section of purchasing agents in both b2b and consumer product and service companies. Purchasing agents were selected because, while others often influence purchases and may even be instrumental in decision making, it is the purchasing agents who usually have the most day-to-day contact with suppliers. Sales managers from b2b and consumer product and service companies were selected because they offered an overall perspective of the entire selling and support process. Finally, marketing managers were included because they are frequently responsible for their company's communication efforts.

One of the first things we wanted to learn from the purchasing agents was whether they saw their suppliers as commodity oriented, that is, providing competitive prices and basic service and support, or customer oriented, working to deliver optimum value and benefit. Customer orientation, which emphasizes relationships and high customer commitment and advocacy, correlates very closely with customer loyalty behavior.

Only 43 percent of the purchasing agents said their suppliers were customer oriented, compared to 73 percent of the sales managers and 71 percent of the marketing managers who thought that purchasing agents would consider them customer oriented. This significant difference was a telling clue into the degree of misinterpretation and misperception between customers and suppliers. The two groups are not speaking the same language, struggling to make each other understood. It's also critical to understanding why the level of customer defection is so high at most companies.

We asked each group to assess the importance and performance of close to 20 elements, or attributes, of value delivery. These included both functional, or rational, attributes and emotional, or relationship, elements. Like the results to our first question, these findings were no less sobering and revealing. Other than pricing, need anticipation, and communication channel availability, purchasing agents consistently gave high attribute ratings far less often than sales and marketing managers

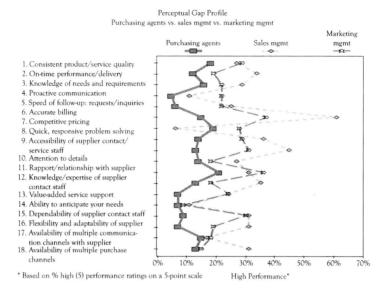

Figure 8.2 Perceptual gaps between purchasing agents, sales managers, and marketing managers

Source: Author.

(Figure 8.2). Many of these differences were in relationship and communication areas, essential in leveraging customer advocacy behavior.

We've frequently found that customers consider the emotional, relationship, and other intangible aspects of value delivery—trust, communication, interactive/collaborative components of service, anticipation of needs, brand equity, and so on—much more important, and more leveraging of behavior, than the functional aspects. Customers tend to see the functional aspects of delivery as more basic and expected, in other words one-dimensional and nondifferentiating.

For companies involved in b2c products or services, the emotional and relationship elements of delivery may represent 70 percent, or more, of what drives supplier choice and loyalty decisions. This, somewhat surprisingly, is similarly true for b2b products and services; so understanding perceptual differences between staff and customers, and recognizing that employees have an emotional and experiential stake in customer value delivery, should be a priority for senior corporate management as well as managers in sales, marketing, and customer service.

When companies are innovative and inclusive with staff, all parties benefit. The company gets more effective employees. Employees like the participation and learning. It enhances their job experiences. Customers like the improved processes. Another key advantage of conducting employee "mirror" research, and one not to be overlooked, is that, in all likelihood, competitors don't have this kind of insight. They're hearing only from the external constituent group, the customers, but not from the equally important representatives and deliverers of value, company employees.

So, recommended prescriptive include

Research field design—When conducting experience research among customers, make certain to include at least one cross-sectional cell of employees. Better still, include enough employees so that segmentation by function, location, tenure, management level, and so on, can be factored into analysis.

Questionnaire mechanics—Ask employees to rate elements of delivery, but with a slight twist. Ask employees to rate the elements of delivery as they think customers will. That way, a "mirroring" protocol has been established, where the enterprise will be able to get a read on how employee perceptions of value sync up with those of customers. Also, and not inconsequentially, include a read on emotional perceptions of experience performance (from both customers and employees).

Spread the news—As an ongoing component of training, customer and employee research results should be shared with employees, either embedded in other instruction programs or as a one-off whenever CX research is conducted.

Notes on Employee Discontent and Sabotage: Implications for CX Management

There is an amply proven, powerful relationship between employee commitment to the company, the brand value proposition, and the customer. For the vast majority of employees, this is the connection to their employers' actual business (financial) and marketplace outcomes.

Yet, when considering, and measuring, the pivotal elements of staff performance and productivity, as we have discussed, most companies are focused principally on employee attitudes around satisfaction, company loyalty, alignment with goals and objectives (such as corporate citizenship), and what they consider to be levels of engagement. These are important, to be sure; but, historically, they only superficially and weakly correlate what employees think and do to actual customer behavior.

To more directly connect employee behavior with customer behavior, we have developed a highly effective suite of research techniques for understanding stakeholder perspectives and decision-making dynamics. For example, customers who actively (frequent informal communication, level of favorability, companies in consideration set, etc.) express their commitment to a supplier can, depending on experiences and perceptions, range from strongly positive (advocates) to negative (saboteurs). Employees, likewise, can significantly impact customer loyalty behavior toward their employer through a range of attitudes and actions on behalf of the brand, company, and customer. These attitudes and actions, similar to customers, range from highly positive to highly negative.

As covered in Chapter 7, our foundation research framework for identifying this is employee ambassadorship. Its intent is to define the most active level of employee commitment to the company's product and service value promise, to the company itself, and to optimizing CX. It is linked to, but distinctive from, the productivity and empowerment elements of employee satisfaction, engagement, and alignment research because, with ambassadorship, emphasis is on building customer bonds, and creating positive transactional and long-term CX through employee interaction.

We most typically concentrate on what drives active, positive, vocal commitment, that is, ambassadorship; however, it is at least equally important to identify where employee indifference and negativism, potentially leading to sabotage attitudes and actions, exist, why they exist, and how they can be mitigated or eliminated. We addressed much of this in the previous chapter, but will review some of the high points here as well.

The Roots of Employee Negativism

To better understand this, we conducted a study through a major polling service among close to 1,200 full-time U.S. employees, 18 years and over. One of our first objectives with these questions was to identify employees' overall commitment level, loyalty, and impression about the company and its ability to earn customers' trust and loyalty. This was accomplished through a series of four simple agree–disagree statements. On two of the questions, commitment to the organization's success and ability to earn customer trust and loyalty, there was fairly high positivism. The two statements that addressed overall impression and loyalty, however, showed significantly greater negativity:

- I am very committed to the success of my employer organization: 78% Yes, 12% No, 10% Not sure
- We consistently earn our customers' trust and loyalty: 76% Yes, 12% No, 12% Not Sure
- I feel very loyal to the organization I currently work for: 69% Yes, 21% No, 10% Not Sure
- I have a very positive impression about the organization I work for: 68% Yes, 22% No, 10% Not Sure

There were definite age-related differences on all of these elements, with younger (18- to 24-year-old) respondents giving lower percentages of "Yes" scores on all measures (see Figure 8.3). For example, on "I am very committed to the success of my employer organization"—63 percent "Yes" by 18- to 24-year-olds compared to 83 percent of those 50 to 64 years and 86 percent by 65+ respondents. Also, there was higher positivism among African Americans and Republicans. There also tended to be some polarizing on these statements based on income: On all measures, those with $34,900 or less income gave lower scores. Finally, on a geographic basis, respondents in the South more frequently gave "Yes" scores on all statements; and female respondents were more loyal to their organizations, had more positive impressions about their organizations, and more frequently said "Yes" to earning customers' trust and loyalty (81% vs. 72%).

Figure 8.3 *Angry young employee*

Source: Internet.

Just as with consumer opinions and decision-making dynamics, informal communication from employees has been proven to have a great deal to do with impressions of an organization, both inside by other employees and outside by customers, vendors, and the general public. We asked if employees tell others how bad their company is as a place to work. A total of 43 percent said they do (7% frequently and 36% sometimes).

Here again, there were differences by age, with greater frequency of saying negative things about their employer among Echo Boomers (49%), significantly lower percentages among Matures, 62+ (25%). Also, negativism was higher among males than females and lower among African Americans, and it was also higher among those with lowest income (48%), and lower among highest income respondents (37%). Finally, negativism was very high among respondents with disabilities (52%) compared to those with no disabilities (40%).

The Potential Impacts of Negativism

In this research, we also wanted to understand the potential effects, inside and outside of the organization, of negatives expressed by employees. We asked respondents if they ever tell others about how bad the products and/or services of their employer are; and over one-third said they do, either frequently (3%) or sometimes (32%).

Demographically, this was higher in the East, and among African American respondents (41%); but, consistent with feelings about their employer, lower among respondents 50 to 64 years (28%) and those over 65 years (25%), but higher among 18- to 24-year-olds (42%). Males were also more negative about their company's products and services than are females (39% vs. 30%). Those who identified their sexual orientation as LGBT also were significantly more negative (60%). There was marked impact of polarity by income level: 44 percent of respondents with $34,900, or less, compared to 31 percent with $75,000+. Finally, there was greater tendency to tell consumers negative things (compared to businesses) and to speak negatively about products compared to services.

To better identify what was behind neutral to negative perceptions of their employer's products and services, we asked respondents why they believed their company does not earn customers' trust and loyalty. The array of key reasons included poor customer interaction and unfair treatment of both customers and employees:

- Profit is only motivation for company (11%)—Told more to consumers (than to businesses)
- Poor customer service (11%)—Told more to consumers (than to businesses)
- Lie to customers (10%)—Almost entirely by Baby Boomers, also more frequently from those with H.S. or less education; told more about products than services
- Inconsistent policies/treat different customers differently (9%)—Strongly from Baby Boomers, also more frequently from those with H.S. or less education; told more about products than services
- Do not treat employees fairly (9%)—Strongly from Baby Boomers, also more frequently from those with H.S. or less education; told more about products than services

Leveraging Employee Positivism

Polar employee positivism, the essence of ambassadorship, is absolutely critical for companies striving to be optimally stakeholder centric. Even though CX management processes may be tightly managed, executing and sustaining them is virtually impossible without the enthusiastic, and real, support of employees. These experiences, and resulting levels of customer loyalty behavior, are greatly influenced by employee interactions. For example, many studies have determined that customers who complain to an organization and have their complaints quickly and satisfactorily resolved tell an average of 5 other people about the good treatment they received, and they tell at least 20 people if they receive poor treatment. Many of these studies were conducted pre-Internet, so the potential for customers to generate negative informal communication (blogs, forums, chat rooms, online communities, rating sites, etc.) is much stronger in today's viral and mobile world.

Service studies have also shown that of the customers who register a complaint, between 54 and 70 percent will do business with the organization again if their complaints are resolved. This figure goes up to 95 percent if the customers feel the complaints are resolved professionally, quickly, and proactively, depending upon both systems and positive employee attitudes and actions.

So, it is both culturally desirable and financially rewarding for organizations to foster employee positivism. Compared to negative word of mouth about their employer as a place to work, our respondents tended to express positives more frequently, which is a very good outcome (for employers and customers) for this research. Overall, 34 percent of the respondents said they frequently tell others how good their company is, and 48 percent sometimes communicated positive messages. Within this positivism, however, it should be noted that the lowest frequent personal positive communication was by 18- to 24-year-olds (24%) and it was highest among those 65+ years (43%), consistent, but in reverse, with age-related expressions of negativism.

Finally, we asked respondents if they tell others how good the products or services of the company they work for are. Encouragingly, a total of 88 percent said they do (38% frequently and 50% sometimes). Employers should be gratified by the marked proclivity of employees to be positive and vocal about their employer's products and/or services, compared to the likelihood of being negative and vocal. Nevertheless, the impact on customer behavior of both positive and negative expression needs to be understood and consistently monitored.

Confronting and Overcoming Employee Negativity

Over the past several years, we've all witnessed situations of major corporations like Wells Fargo, Comcast, and FedEx defending their cultures and laying blame for misdeeds and performance shortfalls on employees. At Comcast, for example, it was senior execs saying that their culture doesn't push employees to deny a customer the right to discontinue service. The incident where this occurred was recorded by a customer and seen by millions of people on YouTube. Contrary to the statements of Comcast executives, rank-and-file customer contact employees affirmed the daily push to both keep customers and to cross sell and upsell them.

More recently, Wells Fargo executives blamed "bad" employees for opening accounts for customers without their permission. Over 5,000 employees were fired—including bankers, managers, and bosses of those managers. As with Comcast, rank-and-file Wells Fargo employees who had been terminated often put the responsibility for Wells Fargo's illegal sales policies squarely on the shoulders of top management, who pressured them to sell. As one of their former bankers noted: "It became a living nightmare. They almost doubled our goals and decreased our incentive pay. It drove me to drink." These are two very public examples of the name-and-blame, which often accompanies disjointed cultures and noncustomer-centric activities. When the Wells Fargo (now former) CEO, stating that the bank has a customer-focused culture, makes a statement like "Everything we do is built on trust. ... It's earned relationship by relationship," one needs to wonder what culture he's actually describing.

Though most employees generally trust the people with whom they work, a recent study by researchers at the London Business School and MIT's Sloan School of Management, among over 11,000 managers from more than 400 companies, found that senior managers trust colleagues in other departments or business units to deliver, as promised or expected, only 10 percent of the time. For instance, only a third of senior managers could correctly identify what the CEO had been communicating about the organization's key priorities. Thus, a vacuum is created, and managers are left to set their own priorities. This becomes an important issue when other departments request information or assistance. In the hustle and bustle of everyday business, managers focus on what is most essential to them and their priorities.

So, there is a lot that drives, or can drive workplace negativity. Much of this has to do with a pervasive lack of trust, evident in every level, department, and location within an enterprise. As discussed, this has tremendous implications for customer value delivery, CX, financial growth, and the employee experience as well. There are several key priorities, which will drive processes, that any organization can apply to both confront and overcome employee negativism. It's, essentially, a three-ingredient recipe.

- *Begin with trust and latitude*—Recognize that employees are as important as customers in achieving company goals. They won't necessarily be consistent, and certainly not perfect, in their actions, Often, this is just a manifestation of applying classic Theory Y principles and putting Theory X management, where employees are tightly managed, in the rearview mirror. For example, it is well known that individual employees of Ritz-Carlton hotels can rectify a guest's problems by giving them up to $2,000 in value. And, by the way, that is $2,000 per incident, not per year, to rescue a guest experience. Compare and contrast that to employees who must consult with, and/or get approval from, managers just to replace a paper clip, which many customers and employees have experienced.
- *Add enablement and empowerment*—Giving employees the tools and training to complete their assigned tasks, as well as ownership for the completion of those tasks, goes a long way to enhancing the experience. Giving them the freedom to use the tools and training, especially for driving greater customer

value, is good for everyone; and it should be baked into their job description. This results in greater individual commitment and contribution.

- *Mix in reward and recognition*—Employees can be compensated, or given perks, as a form of reward for over-and-above performance. They can also be recognized for superior performance, either short term or long term, through devices like promotion, team leadership, and even things as simple as the "plaque on the wall."

Above all, and continuing for a second on the cooking theme, humanity must be the common ingredient for minimizing or eliminating employee apathy and negativism.

Building Humanity Into All Things Stakeholder Related

What makes the focus on humanity so pivotal in customer and employee experience optimization today is that every aspect of stakeholder experience and value delivery is at play. Further, it should be understood that all stakeholders are keenly aware of when humanity is being practiced by an organization and when there is an insufficiency or an absence of the same.

More than a catch phrase, "being human," especially in brand building and leveraging CXs and relationships, has become a buzz phrase or buzz concept. But, there is little that is new or trailblazing in this idea. To understand stakeholders, the enterprise needs to think in human, emotional terms. To make the brand or company more attractive, and have greater impact on stakeholder behavior, there must be an emphasis on creating more perceived value and more personalization. Much of this is, culturally, operationally, and from a communications perspective, what we have been describing as "inside-out advocacy" for years. We can also identify it as stakeholder experience *accueil*, building in growth and mobility opportunities (Figure 8.4), which is explained.

There are a number of ways in which taking a humanistic approach to everything stakeholder related works and directly influences and impacts their behavior. Here are four of them, building from an architectural base.

Figure 8.4 Stakeholder experience growth and opportunity

Source: Internet.

1. **Create a stakeholder-centric human culture and set of processes**

   Evidence of a humanistic, stakeholder-focused enterprise is where values, mission, and vision can be seen, and endorsed, by everyone inside and outside the company. The French have a great word for this—*accueil* (pronounced ack-key)—which means openness, acceptance, welcoming, and receptivity. It sets up as a major distinction with most Theory X, micromanaged, repressive cultures and array of customer processes.

   Accueil can be seen in transactions and relationships with companies like Southwest Airlines, Trader Joe's, Wegmans, and USAA. As pointed out by books like *Conscious Capitalism* and *Firms of Endearment*, and as identified in multiple experience effectiveness studies, stakeholder-centric company cultures, supported by customer-centric processes and positive employee–customer interactions, also perform at consistently attractive financial levels over extended periods of time.

2. **Create experiences that are proactively human engineered**

   Within customer-related processes, experiences need to be designed, engineered, or reengineered, so that authentic humanity is built in. With the dramatic increases in digital transactions, long-distanced relationships, and marketing automation, this has become an increasing challenge. However, this is also where the concepts of accueil can be observed.

More than Six Sigma–type rational and functional quality, it is the authentic warmth and openness that most customers desire from vendors, even when contact is minimal. Human-engineered experiences also require that measurement techniques be sensitive to the components that drive, or detract from, what customers get from their vendor relationships. Most companies collect small and big data to do more targeted marketing selling, and use metrics like customer satisfaction, indices, Net Promoter Score (NPS) and/or Customer Effort Score (CES) to reward or punish employees. In fact, employees need to be active participants in the design of CXs, in part because it enhances their own experiences.

3. **Create human emotions and memories in transactions and relationships**

Today, delivery of functional and tangible elements of value, even at superior levels, are little more than experience table stakes. We often speak of the Daniel Kahneman "peak-end rule," where subconscious positive and negative experience emotions yield the memories, which drive downstream customer behavior. This psychologically based approach is a critical differentiator for companies to successfully bringing the human touch to transactions and relationships.

A couple of years ago, Bridget Duffy, MD, who is the Chief Medical Officer of Vocera Communications, wrote an insightful *CustomerThink* blog post about how emotional connections, coming out of a culture of humanity, can drive customer loyalty behavior and company growth. From my perspective, the value of creating positive emotions can't be stated much better than she did:

Customers choose service providers based on personal experiences, trusted relationships and valued recommendations. To understand customer needs and expectations, organizations must first map the gaps in efficiency plus empathy. Market leaders must provide services and use technologies that restore empathy to the customer experience. Dr. Duffy might just as easily have been describing the necessity for building humanity into employee experiences.

4. Create human connections between employee ambassadors and customers

Advertising and promotion, in and of themselves, generate little trust. Outbound communication is principally designed to be likable and relatable. B2b and b2c consumers trust humans more than companies or institutions. Smart companies operate as "real people," with employees working to provide value to customers.

In humanistic organizations, employees at all levels, and in all functions, understand how their work and actions impact customer perception of experiences. If employee ambassadorship is an extension of the company's customer-related DNA, then it is employees who embody accueil.

It is not nearly enough for employees to be engaged. Humanistic experience is achieved when employees are armed and enabled to deliver on the brand promise. The technology and tools can't replace real-time passion, or genuine commitment to the organization, brand, and customers.

Often, it is employees who are the real, flexible experience engineers. As needed, they can personalize interactions by treating each customer differently, and even the same customer differently, if the experience context is different (something I've labeled as customer "divisibility," which is also somewhat data dependent).

As a concluding thought, it's important to point out that executing in all these areas requires enterprise and functional leadership that understands what human centricity means in customer relationships and overall perceived experience value. As Dr. Duffy stated in her blog, companies:

must focus on building connections and relationships into all aspects of the organization—from executive leadership to front-line staff—so that from the first impression to the last, people feel a connection. Going beyond customer service to creating a real emotional connection to a product, service or company will drive market differentiation, customer loyalty and growth.

We're in violent agreement here. Accueil, a sense of actual humanity in all aspects of CX delivery, matters a great deal.

Positivity and Inside-Out Advocacy: Creating and Sustaining a Culture of Inclusive Stakeholder Centricity and Customer Loyalty

We can all pretty much agree that most of what drives customer loyalty behavior begins as a result of *transparency, relevance, authenticity, and trust*, four essential elements in the way customers see suppliers through their own value lens and set of personal experiences. Inside the company, this is strongly influenced by customer-focused touch point and support processes, corporate leadership and culture, and employee interaction. As Professor Peter Fader, codirector of the Customer Analytics Initiative at The Wharton School, has stated (in his recent book, *Customer Centricity*):

> Customer centricity can help you create a passionate, committed customer base that will spread word of your company's attributes to potential new customers. Customer centricity can improve the way your customers view you—even as those customers pour more money into your coffers. But most important, it will also generate profits—for the long term.

There's much that needs to be considered and understood about what creates, builds, and sustains customer loyalty, not the least of which is how stakeholder behavior is measured, internalized, and acted upon.

Where's the Focus? What Is the Result?

Corporate executives are—or should be—always concerned about what drives customer commitment and advocacy behavior. They tend to believe that as customers gain experience with their enterprises, entirely through people, products, and services, this will result in deeper relationships and engagement. However, organizational structure and culture, the ways companies use available customer data, and the positioning and messaging companies create, are no less important. Neither are the focus on employee commitment, and the design and provision of enriching experiences for them; and corporate executives ought to be as concerned with employee behavior, especially on behalf of customers.

This is a time when customers and employees have grown increasingly skeptical about organizational focus on their personal and individual benefit relative to corporate self-interest, and also an awareness that the traditional "push" communication delivered from companies does not resonate, penetrate, or influence as in years past. In any form or fashion, relevance, authenticity, and trust must be delivered at every touch point. This absolutely requires that the meld between culture, messaging, and stakeholder experience be as seamless as possible.

If companies want customers to advocate for them on the outside, and employees to serve as ambassadors both inside and outside the company, the advocacy process needs to begin with the right culture, the right messages, the right media, the right processes, and the right strategic experience creation from within the organization. Banks, airlines, wireless telecoms, retailers, insurance companies, realtors, utilities, b2b companies, and even government agencies feel compelled to express the strength of their focus and allegiance to customers, particularly in areas of service and relationship-building, often as statements and manifestos of commitment. Are the words companies use true differentiators of perceived benefit and value, and customer loyalty and engagement delivered through employees, with the employees serving as active partners in that delivery, or are they just reflections of expected basics of performance, and often disbelieved?

When customers are considering alternative suppliers and/or making final purchase decisions, it is now becoming well understood that the principal, previously underappreciated choice criteria are the intangible, emotional, relationship components of value. Often, much of what is tangible, functional, and rational—value elements such as quality, reliability, timeliness, and price—are seen as one-dimensional and nondifferentiating "table stakes." For instance, Verizon can say "Better matters" in its advertising, but are customers and employees in agreement with that, experience-wise?

Advocacy and Ambassadorial Creation Templates

Advocacy and ambassadorship clearly monetize. So, it's important for organizations to understand that customer commitment and advocacy behavior can result in one of two ways. The first way, which we identify as the generation of "inside-out" customer commitment and advocacy, is where companies endeavor to manage and influence attitudes and perceptions of customers (and prospects), as well as where, how, and when communication takes place.

Though there are many thought leaders who offer insights into how organizations can produce benefit for stakeholders through culture and value, Glen Urban, professor of marketing at MIT, initially outlined this very well in his book *Don't Just Relate—Advocate!: A Blueprint for Profit in the Era of Customer Power*. Two other books *The Experience Economy: Work Is Theater & Every Business a Stage* and *Authenticity: What Consumers Really Want*, both by James Gilmore and B. Joseph Pine II, and a fourth book that we previously introduced, *Firms of Endearment*, by marketing professors Jagdish Sheth, Raj Sisodia, and David Wolfe(plus its successor, *Conscious Capitalism*), did an even better job of explaining how organizations can create and institutionalize superior experiences and value for all stakeholders.

Particularly in *Firms of Endearment*, the authors identified elements of *stakeholder relationship management* (rather than a traditional stockholder and stock price-focused) model for creating a strategic and emotional bond between the enterprise and its customers. Importantly, they recognized that the "invention" of the World Wide Web (by British software engineer Tim Berners-Lee) in 1991 became a seminal, high-frequency communication enabler, also fundamentally changing the balance of decision-influencing and informational power to the b2c and b2b consuming masses. It also changed the form and amount of interaction between peers. Most critically, as it impacts stakeholders, this has forced organizations to act with greater and greater openness and customer sensitivity; and it also spurred more active consideration of the role and behavior of employees in driving CX and delivering customer value.

Advocacy Building Results in the Real World

Skepticism, information availability, and economic instability have combined to change the landscape of product and service decision making, probably forever. As b2b and b2c consumers seek more meaning from everything—their work, their relationships, even the companies with which they do business, the result is that organizations will be perceived as partners to the degree with which they can align their products, services, values, and culture with the needs of stakeholders. Very few companies have been able to do this, either at creation or through transformation; however, those that have succeeded are true customer advocacy performance exemplars.

Sheth, Sisodia, and Wolfe called such organizations "humanistic" companies, which seek to maximize their value to each group of stakeholders, not just to shareholders. These companies, which the authors refer to as "FoEs," have succeeding in aligning (not just balancing) the interests of all stakeholders. They are focused on employee hiring, training, and teamwork, and empower employees to optimize, and "humanize," CXs. They work in partnership with suppliers.

For the authors, a truly great company is one that makes the world a better place because it exists. Simple as that. In the book, which was published in 2007, the authors have identified about 30 companies, from multiple industries, that met their criteria. They included CarMax, BMW, Costco, Harley-Davidson, IKEA, JetBlue, Johnson & Johnson, New Balance, Patagonia, Timberland, Trader Joe's, UPS, Wegmans—and Southwest Airlines. Had the book been written a bit later, it's likely that Zappos would have made their list as well.

The Winning "Inside-Out" Advocacy Formula: Customer-Focused Self-Awareness and Self-Regulation

How did they do it? By what magic did these companies achieve such stellar results? According to the authors, it begins with "emotionally intelligent" management, based on ideas offered in the 1995 and 1998 books by Daniel Coleman. This is principally the ability to be self-aware and self-regulating, emotionally and socially, a capability the authors recognize as being absent or ignored in most organizational cultures, even those that are otherwise fairly stakeholder centric. However, it is a necessary component of leadership development at all levels, and in all functions, of any company. Without it, the authors assert, the tone of the enterprise and its driving core culture features—how much people give and want to give, and how much they care about the enterprise and its other stake-holders—will be impaired, yielding low morale and interpersonal consideration, and high levels of conflict and stress. The result is that business effectiveness, that is, bottom-line outcomes, will suffer.

Also recognized is the power of communications, both inside and outside of the organization. As the *Firms of Endearment* authors stated:

> Instead of business-controlled monologues, the marketplace is now dominated by conversations. People talk to each other as never before about the companies they work for, buy from and invest in. This is forcing companies to operate with greater transparency. But that is not a problem for companies with nothing to hide, as firms of endearment have discovered. Transparency helps customers, employees, and other stakeholders develop trust in a company. It has proven to be effective as a motivating force among employees.

Much of the creation of trust, per the authors, has to do with the employees who create differentiated CXs, and who have desirable experiences created for them as well. The relevant point made is that, beginning with the hiring process, firms that create strong bonds with their customers select employees based both on skill set fit and also fit within the culture and customer orientation. L.L. Bean looks for employees who are dedicated outdoor types. Whole Foods and Trader Joe's look for people who like dealing with food (and people) as a key part of their lives. Harley-Davidson looks for new staffers who are into motorcycles.

Measuring the Advocacy Behavior Impact of "Inside-Out" Elements

In targeted customer advocacy research, we can identify, based on the specific perceived value and CX circumstances, which elements will most significantly drive positive and negative customer behavior. Studies in retail banking, see Figure 8.5 for example, showed that some key staff-related service elements—follow-up and making proactive recommendations—could drive more positive advocacy, while timely service delivery and

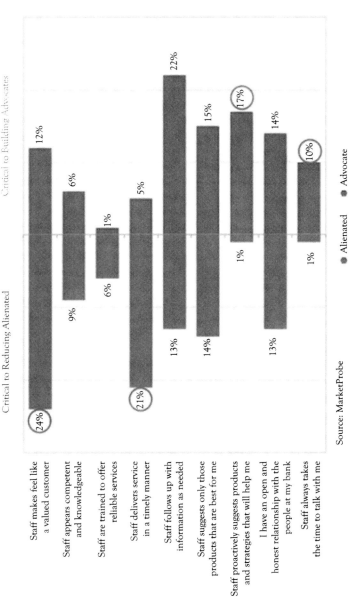

Figure 8.5 Influence of employee interaction

Source: Beyond Philosophy (www.beyondphilosophy.com).

making customers feel valued at the bank, if not performed well from the customer's perspective, could create more negativism.

Building on the discussion of employee negativism covered in this chapter, resulting customer disaffection, based on our findings, can result in diversion of available customer monies to secondary and tertiary banks, disinclination to take new bank products, and even potential churn.

From a more process-based and experience-based banking customer standpoint, knowledge of employees, followed by waiting time and branch aesthetics, were seen as positive branch advocacy drivers, while waiting time, as a double-edged sword, could create negative customer behavior if not seen as being performed well. Transaction completion time, another key process-based employee-centric element, could also have negative downstream behavioral leverage.

Important Stakeholder Centricity Guidelines

Finally, the *Firms of Endearment* authors identified some unique operating traits among its chosen examples of customer-driven cultural excellence:

- Decision making is decentralized, but in ways, which actually increase the visibility and influence of key executives throughout the company.
- Frontline staff, that is, those dealing directly with customers, are paid at higher rates compared to their peers at other companies.
- A cornerstone of the book, these companies spend far less on marketing and advertising than their competitors, depending more on their "inside-out advocacy" and employee ambassadorship creation abilities to drive outside-in customer advocacy.

This last point, of course, is particularly important and has major impact on most organizations and their customer-related budgets. Truly excellent companies rely on advocating customers, ambassadorial employees, and engaged suppliers—positive communication offline and online through social media—to spread the word, reducing the need for advertising to build awareness and public relations to build image and reputation. Google, for instance, became one of the world's most valuable brands without any advertising. The authors note that one of their example companies, Jordan's, a major regional furniture retailer, spends only about 2 percent of gross revenue on marketing, compared to 7 percent for the average furniture retailing chain, yet generates square-foot sales that are five times that of most furniture stores.

To create an organizational culture that is loved and respected by all stakeholder groups, three primary elements are required: **a strategic vision, a set of core values,** and **perceived energy and perseverance**. This vision, a common theme to all companies studied in *Firms of Endearment*, is based on maximizing creation of value. The binding force for keeping these companies focused and centered is the set of values to which they commit. The energy, visible to customers as they interact with the company, and to employees as they go about their work, is a reflection of the passion and commitment they generate.

One of my favorite movie quotes sums up what can differentiate companies as humanistic, values driven, and stakeholder focused. In *A League of Their Own*, manager Jimmy Dugan (Tom Hanks) says to Dottie Hinson, his star player (Geena Davis), who is leaving the team because playing was no longer fun and had gotten too hard: "It's supposed to be hard. If it wasn't hard, everyone would do it. The hard ... is what makes it great." "Hard" is also the discipline to take the enterprise culture beyond the antecedent bounds of employee engagement, satisfied customers, and the Service-Profit Chain.

Few would claim that creating and sustaining stakeholder centricity from the inside out is easy, simple, or quick. But the results can be great and are more than worth the effort. Though the issue of culture's morale and performance impact is extremely important, the focus does need to be on the experience of both the employee and the customer.

Management pundits like Peter Drucker (and Thomas Lloyd, Edgar Shein, Jack Welch, and others) have been quoted as saying that "culture eats strategy for breakfast." In fact, none of them ever made that exact statement; but there is ample proof that a cohesive, collaborative, caring, stakeholder-centric culture will continue to be a priority for organizations seeking to drive security, financial success, productivity, performance, and other positive outcomes.

CHAPTER 9

The Employee Life Cycle of the Future and Ambassadorship in Practice

For Some Time, It's Been Understood That Customers Have a Defined Life Cycle. ...

A few years ago, findings of the Chartered Institute of Marketing (CIM) in the United Kingdom, namely, that less than 1 out of 10 British adults believed that relational marketing gave them more value than the suppliers providing the benefits and that they also don't want these organizations driving the relationship shouldn't surprise many. Customers are savvy, fickle, demanding, and value directed. They're certainly intelligent enough to know the difference between a program with components that create genuine value and one that's little more than a giveaway or an old-fashioned snake oil repeat sales pitch.

Irrespective of size, it's essential for all companies, whether online or offline, b2b or b2c, or profit or nonprofit, to understand customer life stages. Though becoming less prevalent, most organizations still don't look at the complete spectrum of a customer's life, especially from an emotional perspective. Just as relatively few companies have developed algorithms and processes for estimating lifetime customer revenue value, so also few companies realize how their experience and value initiatives, programs, and processes have to be modified depending on the customer's life stage.

Companies in industries like banking, telecom, cable, and automotive, for instance, are still rather notorious for devoting large proportions of their marketing budgets to new customer acquisition, which some of them like to label as "conquest" or "capture," and then treating customers pretty passively once in the fold.

More recently, observers have witnessed the furious and expensive prospecting for new customers among e-commerce companies, only to lose them, principally through poor follow-up, continuity of communication, and service, at an almost equally furious pace. Numerous consulting and research companies have noted how attraction activity contrasts with the low and benign level of service these customers tend to receive after coming onboard. These are clear continuity breakdowns as customers move through their life stages.

Experience and value creation should be viewed more proactively, as a never-ending process that embraces mutually beneficial relationships for all customers, that is, past, present, and potential, and internal, intermediate, and external, creating not only enticements to become customers, but also anticipatory deterrents to risk or churn. Most particularly, it makes perfect sense (at least to me) that companies have either programs or elements in their overall experience management and activity plans that address what is required and desired for each customer and at each life stage.

As we see them, there are three fundamental phases of a complete customer life cycle: *Targeting/Acquisition*, *Retention/Loyalty*, and *Lost/Won-Back*. This translates, as covered earlier in the book, to seven stages of a customer's life with a supplier:

- Suspect
- Prospect (Active/Developmental)
- Customer (New/Recovered)
- Retained/Loyal Customer
- At-Risk Customer (Attrition)
- Defected/Lost Customer
- Recovered/Won Back Customer

Here's how the life stages work. Taking, as an example, a town with two bakeries, the suspect stage would begin when a potential customer first desires baked goods, such as a delicious crème-filled doughnut, fruit pie, strawberry shortcake, or specialty artisan bread. That desire may come on its own, or it may have been encouraged or stimulated by one or both of the bakeries advertising and promoting their tasty wares.

The potential customer then becomes a prospect, going through a screening process, sorting through perceptions of each bakery's image and reputation, array and quality of desired products and services, awareness of prices, and other information, such as referrals, advertising, or promotional materials. The prospect is considered either active or developmental, depending upon how strong the purchase desire for baked goods is at this stage.

Then, the final bakery selection is made, and the prospect becomes a new customer. The bakery's complete value proposition—personalized service and communication, product quality and range, and price, to cite a few of the key elements—creates a level of emotional commitment within the customer. If that commitment is strong enough, the new customer will make repeat purchases over time and become a retained/loyal customer, eventually becoming an advocate for, and bonding with, the preferred bakery. Frequency, variety, and volume of purchase will mark the customer's long-term value to the bakery.

If any negative perception develops regarding an important aspect of value—product quality, array, price, communication, or service—the new customer or the retained/loyal customer can, or will, enter an attrition mode and become an at-risk customer. This is where the bakery should be most aware of customer perceptions, because the undermining of perceived value is the strongest contributor to exit or churn.

Should the customer's problems or complaints with the chosen bakery not be resolved, or if the problems or complaints become stronger than the benefits provided, then the customer is lost, or defected, most likely to the other bakery in town, if the desire for baked goods is still strong.

Assuming the bakery is like most companies, once the customer has been lost, rather minimal resources or effort will be devoted to either understanding the reasons for the customer's exit or winning the customer back. Speaking personally, this is something I've experienced over and over again. Let's be positive, though. Let's say the bakery does know the customer on a one-to-one basis, does make an effort to know why the customer left, does have a process to win the customer back, and does succeed in getting the customer to return. Then, the customer could be considered recovered or won back. During this win back process, the customer might be viewed as a prospect again, especially if the value proposition needs to be completely reexpressed.

Most bakeries, again like most online and bricks-and-mortar companies, typically set their customer behavior goals around increased spending and purchase frequency, and to increased profitability and market share. They do this by offering something of presumed positive value so that the customer will have a stronger emotional relationship and identification with the products and the bakery itself. But that's where the majority of programs begin and end. They tend to be rather one-dimensional, rather than push for advocacy and bonding.

These programs should also function as a referral vehicle to attract new customers. This can happen in two ways. The new customer or the retained/loyal customer will offer positive word of mouth to suspects and prospects, that is, friends, colleagues, and relatives. The other way is that what the bakery offers in products or relationship is so strong and attractive that noncustomers learn of it and are drawn in. Their experiences, assuming they're positive, then serve to repeat this process.

How does the bakery's experience program respond when the customer becomes at risk? If it's an organic and kinetic program, the bakery will have collected and interpreted sufficient, actionable insights during its customers' earlier life stages. If service or product problems surface, the bakery should be able to have intensified contact and communication with these customers to stabilize the bond and commitment. The bakery may also offer some type of value incentive to the at-risk customer to help reestablish the relationship.

As we've often said, relationship dynamics, especially when the customer has been lost or defected, are quite different than when the customer is active. At the point of exit, the customer has become emotionally detached from the bakery. There is no longer sufficient value in product or service for the customer to remain.

Especially if the customer has had high volume and/or frequent purchase activity, once the customer has been identified as lost, the customer-centric bakery has to do two things: (1) Find out why the customer has left, and (2) have communication techniques and processes in place to help drive recovery.

If the root cause of departure has been a product or service issue, restating the value proposition and offering some "please come back" incentives may (or may not) be enough to reestablish the relationship. If the customer has moved, had a lifestyle change (such as going on a diet, or learning that he/she has a pastry allergy), or been lured away by lower prices, any recovery effort will probably not be worthwhile or successful. If won back, the customer is recovered.

The kind of focus on customer segmentation by life stage almost absolutely necessitates that companies have a single, integrated view of customers that's enterprisewide. Do they? A study by Forrester Research showed that while 92 percent of companies say this is critical (44%) or very important (48%), only 12 percent of companies say they have it fully (2%) or somewhat (10%). So, for most companies, having a relationship and experience program that flexes to accommodate each stage of a customer's life will be a challenge at minimum. For even more companies, having a program that includes lost customers is nonexistent.

Companies' relationship programs tend to focus principally on attracting new customers or rewarding customers who are either new or who spend a lot or spend frequently, mostly in the short term. That's fine and completely appropriate, but it makes secondary many customer groups and life stages, which may offer attractive revenue and profit opportunity. It may, as well, completely bypass some customer groups—notably those who are at risk or defected.

For those who doubt whether this life cycle concept works equally well for online, as well as offline, customers, consider this: The "rules" for stages of online customer behavior are pretty much the same as for offline customers—but online life stages can sometimes occur with almost the speed of a key stroke.

Several centuries ago, Takeda Shingen, a samurai general in medieval Japan, wrote: "A person with deep far-sightedness will survey both the beginning and the end of a situation, and continually consider its every facet as important." We believe the same kind of thinking should be applied to customer life stages. Every life stage represents attractive potential revenue and profit, and also risk, as well as learning, which affects the other stages. Every life stage is important.

... . Well, So Do Employees. ...

For some time, it has been understood that when purchasing a product or service, consumers are essentially "hiring" a supplier to get a job done.

The same can be said of employees. They can hire desired employers, and if things don't turn out as expected, employees can "fire" their employer, sometimes quietly, sometimes noisily, departing.

Clayton Christensen, a professor of business administration at Harvard Business School, has identified this trend in his book *Competing Against Luck: The Story of Innovation and Customer Choice*. As he noted, the new employee has accepted the job, but he or she has also accepted, or hired, the company. The goal is to make career and life, that is, experiential, progress, so making the right decision at the outset is extremely important. As explained by Christensen, this is considerably more than title and salary, which are just the very basic functional components of the job. It must include both emotional and social components of value, more nuanced elements of the job experience, which are of at least equal importance to the employee.

According to TechTarget, employee life cycle can be defined as follows: "The employee life cycle (ELC, also sometimes spelled as *employee lifecycle*) is a HR-based model that identifies stages in employees' careers to help guide their management and optimize associated processes." In many respects, then, the employee life cycle is similar to the customer life cycle.

Specific employee life cycle models vary but consistent employee life cycle stages often include:

Recruitment: This stage includes all the processes leading up to and including the hiring of a new employee. E-recruitment software may be used to automate some of the selection process, for example, filtering applications and resumes for requirements. This is rather analogous to suspect and prospect stages of the customer life cycle.

Onboarding: In this relatively brief stage, the employee is added to the organization's identity and access management system. The stage includes ensuring that the employee has access to any applications and systems that are required for his job.

Orientation: In this stage, the employee settles into the job, integrates with the corporate culture, familiarizes himself/herself with co-workers and management, and generally establishes his/her role within the organization.

Career planning: During the planning stage, the employee and management collaboratively develop objectives and goals. Personality profile assessments are sometimes used in conjunction with an evaluation of the employee's performance to date. This may be periodically reassessed, somewhat dependent on employee performance and desires, and available paths within the enterprise.

Career development: In this stage, the employee matures in his/her role in the organization. Professional development frequently involves additional training and/or exposure. The challenges in this stage are employee engagement and retention.

Termination: In this final stage, sometimes referred to as "transition," the employee leaves the organization. The specific processes are somewhat dependent upon whether the departure is the result of voluntary resignation, firing, or retirement. However, in any case, off-boarding is a feature—the employee is removed from the company's system. Many organizations schedule exit interviews in an attempt to get useful input from the departing employee.

What should be emphasized in the HR-based models of employee life cycle, especially in Career Development, is how the job experience is, or can be, enhanced with a focus on commitment to the customer, product and service value proposition, and to the organization itself. This transcends the traditional emphasis on concepts of employee engagement and retention initiatives practiced by most companies.

Does Employee Loyalty = Customer Loyalty? And, Did It Ever?

Many HR and corporate leaders consider employee loyalty (often conflated with employee satisfaction and engagement) a crucial element in any customer loyalty or customer experience (CX) program. They believe that without requisite employee loyalty, plus alignment with goals and productivity, the chances of a customer loyalty program succeeding are, in the long run, not very good. The equation and presumption of employee loyalty = customer loyalty has been around for decades, but is employee loyalty, alone, really enough to drive desired customer behavior?

In the United States, employment rates are high. Staffing and staff retention have become critical priorities. There are few industries not experiencing high pressure on finding, and keeping, qualified personnel. It has been suggested that companies should apply a marketing perspective to the challenge of attracting and retaining employees. The logic goes like this: You have a product, called a "job" that is being sold to a customer, called an "employee." When you think about employee loyalty as a marketing challenge, the questions to ask are what actions should be taken to turn prospective employees into new hires, and once that happens, what actions and initiatives are required to turn new hires into longer-term employees and ultimately, staunch company advocates and ambassadors?

With every employee life cycle comes predictable crisis points when staff defection risks are greatest. These crises often have, as well, influences on customer behavior. The better a company can predict and plan for these job experience–related stress points, the more chance risk and defection can be prevented and the employee can be retained and refocused on delivering value. Three common crisis periods for employees are:

1. New hire hysteria. This condition can be brought on by a number of "new job" circumstances including underwhelming assignments, friction with a new boss, or an unexpectedly heavy workload. It doesn't take much for the new employee to call a headhunter or even the old employer and say the four deadly words: "I made a mistake." Solution: Pair the new recruit with an experienced associate who can help guide the employee through this difficult transition time. In addition, provide a new hire with in-depth orientation to acclimate, and assimilate, the individual into the company.

2. Promotion peril. A employee is vulnerable to defection when he or she is ready for a promotion but a slot is unavailable. Ambitious, upwardly mobile employees "waiting" for promotions are ripe for the picking from competitors who are only too happy to give them that next step up on the ladder. Solution: Buy some extra time by putting the employee in a special project role (2–3 months in duration) that recognizes his or her achievements. In the interim, find that promotion slot!

3. Boredom blues. The most productive employees typically don't tolerate boredom well. No promotion on the horizon? No new project to look forward to? New jobs outside your company will look more and more attractive. Solution: Find out what specific areas most interest the employee and find ways to tailor at least some of the bored employee's assignments around those areas.

But managing the employee life cycle is more than simply managing employee loyalty crisis points. It's about laying a strong foundation that helps build the employee experience and preempt risk and defection issues before they even occur. That means creating a stakeholder-centric culture within the organization that nurtures employee commitment and ambassadorship from the moment the new hire walks through the door and throughout the life span of the employee. The good news is that employees, by their very nature, desire to part of something bigger. As *Fortune* magazine columnist Thomas Stewart has said, "Human beings want to pledge allegiance to something. The desire to belong is a foundation value, underlying all others."

In Chapter 1, detail was offered for the nine "best practices," generated for *Customer WinBack*, my 2001 book cowritten with Jill Griffin, for generating employee behavior, which extends beyond loyalty to contribution and commitment. They are summarized in the following text. These appear top down, but they can come from any management or supervisory level:

1. Build a climate of trust—that works both ways.
2. Train, train, train, and cross-train.
3. Make sure each employee has a career path.
4. Provide frequent evaluations and reviews.
5. Seek to inform, seek to debrief.
6. Recognize and reward initiative.
7. Ask employees what they want.
8. By all means, have fun.
9. Hire the right employees in the first place.

To build more of the first best practice, employee trust and empowerment, into the company culture, organizations would be wise to consider the following:

- Insure staff trust and empowerment are key values in the firm's mission and vision statements.
- Practice effective storytelling.
- Create company rites and rituals that help reinforce the rewards of employee trust.
- Maintain a free flow of information between management and staff to reinforce the trust factor and help prevent negative communication and gossip.
- Actively expose all employees to customers' perception of experience value.
- Teach senior managers the importance of "walking the talk" and inspiring employee trust.

Employees often complain that while they are working harder than ever, their contributions or thoughts on anything beyond their immediate jobs are rarely sought. Says an employee in a communications company:

> I have lots of ideas, but I'm not one of the inner circle of people making those decisions and don't know how to approach them. They all sit in adjacent offices and seem to talk more to each other than anyone else. There's little reaching out to a broad array of employees for ideas and input.

This is both a challenge and an opportunity. Employees who feel underutilized, nonempowered, nonenabled, or ignored become unproductive and often seek job fulfillment elsewhere. Bringing all employees into closer proximity with customers on a regular basis, for example, is a great way for them to be part of the action of the stakeholder experience ball game. Southwest Airlines, often singled out as an exemplar of employee cross-training around CX enhancement, also succeeds in this endeavor by having employees make a positive difference in their own experience as well. Employees need to be more than just loyal and they need to be more than engaged. They need to be ambassadors: committed to the organization itself, to the value proposition represented by its products and services, and to its customers.

And, Throughout the Employee Life Cycle, Ambassadorship Is Entirely Based on Job Experience (Or, It Should Be. ...)

What motivates, or demotivates, an employee's actions in moving along the career path has much to do with where that individual exists in the job life cycle. Is that employee loyal? Is that employee at risk? Is that employee's experience powerful and positive enough that ambassadorial behavior results?

Here, that is, career path and work fulfillment, are two of those key instances where job satisfaction and engagement are not nearly sufficient, and, as concepts, they have probably outlived their useful shelf life. Per Christensen, it is these core intrinsic experience factors, those that are emotional and remain in the employee's memory, which predominate. On the job, employees need to be constantly asking emotionally based questions:

1. Am I being challenged in my work?
2. Am I learning?
3. Am I respected by my peers?
4. Am I respected by my boss?
5. Does the company have a mission (and vision) I can support?
6. Am I free to make my own decisions on issues affecting my work?
7. Am I positive about my career path within the organization?
8. Do I truly believe in the customer value of the company's products and services?
9. Am I informally telling others about my positive (or negative) job-related feelings?

Intrinsic motivation, and the degree of emotional positivism and negativism derived from the employee's work, identify if all of the previous questions are being answered in ways that both the employee and employer desire. Career and job experience can follow ebbs and flows very similar to CX. They directly impact the employee life cycle. The sooner organizations, and particularly HR and senior management, recognize this and begin to think and execute from this premise, the more effectively they can create stakeholder centricity and employee ambassadorship.

Three Examples of Employee Ambassadorship in Practice

Delivering Unique, Attractive (Even Branded) CX Lagniappe: With the Help of Employee Ambassadorship, Any Company Can Do This

My colleague Bob Thompson (CEO of the *CustomerThink* CX portal) recently wrote an informative, timely blog post on strategies companies can use to make CX a competitive advantage—and how most neither measure experience nor compete on it—and that put me in mind of a line of discussion around CX *lagniappe*. Other stakeholder experience consultants, myself included, have all been exposed to, and reported on, what lagniappe can do for any company, irrespective of size, industry, or location.

For those not familiar with the term, let's quickly revisit what it is. When my wife and I visited Southern Louisiana, we noticed that a lot of retailers differentiated themselves by doing a little something extra for customers. One experience that stood out was our dinner at Restaurant R'evolution at the Royal Sonesta Hotel in the French Quarter. If you don't order dessert (we didn't, because we were too full from the appetizer and main course), the waiter brings a red Peruvian jewelry box. Each drawer has a different little candy, cookie, pastry, or other confection inside. The treat is cost-free, delightful, and memorable. It's experience lagniappe.

This so impressed me that having read Chip Bell's great book *Sprinkles: Creating Awesome Experiences Through Innovative Service*, I wrote to him about it. Bell then posted a wonderful *CustomerThink* blog about the concept after visiting Restaurant R'evolution himself. Here's the reality about experience lagniappe: It isn't new. The idea of providing customers with a little extra value has been known for over a century. In the Merriam-Webster page defining lagniappe, here's the description it received:

"We picked up one excellent word," wrote Mark Twain in **Life on the Mississippi** (1883), "a word worth traveling to New Orleans to get; a nice limber, expressive, handy word—'lagniappe'. … It is Spanish, so they said." Twain encapsulated the history of "lagniappe" quite nicely. English speakers learned the word from French-speaking Louisianians, but they in turn had adapted it from the American Spanish word la ñapa.

Twain went on to describe how New Orleansians completed shop transactions by saying "Give me something for lagniappe," to which the shopkeeper would respond with "a bit of licorice-root, … a cheap cigar or a spool of thread."

Lagniappe hasn't seen much acceptance outside of South Louisiana, and it certainly hasn't caught on in other areas of the country. Customers would be hard-pressed to find it consistently in experiences they receive from most b2b and b2c organizations.

Bell has written that:

We are reaching the limits of value-added service (taking what customers expect and adding more). It is time for value-unique. And while there is an obvious ceiling on generosity, there is no limit to the ways to be ingenious.

This extends the narrower realm of service to all elements of CX. Whether, as Bob Thompson discussed, the strategy focuses on touch point improvements, seamless customer-focused journey, or delivering stand-out, branded experiences (think Zappos, Trader Joe's, Wegmans, Southwest Airlines, Zane's Cycles, The Container Store, Metro, or Umpqua Bank), any company can do experience lagniappe.

How? Well, start here:

1. Make the small investment in enhancing employee experience, and have them focus on customer value. Empower and enable employees to be more mindful of delivering what customers need and want, irrespective of level of function within the company.
2. Make the small investment to identify and understand what customers value on an emotional, not just physical, level, and determine what is memorable about the experience.
3. Overpromise and overdeliver, consistently, on experience.

4. Where customers and experience are concerned, think "human," that is, TD Bank's "Bank Human Again" marketing campaign.

5. Recognize that company and product/service image and reputation are integral to customer perception of value.

6. Work to build and institutionalize customer value delivery, that is, conscious customer centricity through employee ambassadorship, into the enterprise DNA.

Be distinctive in value provision. Experience lagniappe is out there. It doesn't require that much in the way of financial investment, innovation, or ingenuity. Just a willingness to "think customer" and consistently execute just a bit outside the box. I've written about Vernon Hill, who founded Commerce Bank in the United States and Metro Bank in the United Kingdom. He understands lagniappe. From my blog covering what Metro does to distinguish its banking experience: "What further distinguishes Metro are some of the little touches—free lollipops on the counter for the kids, and water bowls for customers' dogs."

As Hill has noted:

> There are always some economic case studies that prove cutting costs or raising fees makes sense. But there's never been one that says being nice to dogs or being open seven days a week makes sense. It's about building fans of your service, not customers. Great companies build fans who become loyal, remain loyal, and bring their friends.

Lagniappe works, for both customers and employees, and it is hoped that the content of *Employee Ambassadorship* has been able to demonstrate how a concept like this extends to enriching the employee experience.

Employee Ambassadorship Lives at Iron Hill Brewery: A Warm, Pre-Christmas Customer Advocacy Story

It had been uncommonly warm where we live in the Delaware Valley a couple of Decembers ago. Taking advantage of the rare mild late fall weather, one Sunday my wife and I decided to spend a relaxing afternoon strolling along the Brandywine River in downtown Wilmington, Delaware, and then have a nice dinner at a high-end seafood restaurant. We watched kids and parents in T-shirts and shorts ice skating at the Riverfront rink, and petted cute dogs being walked along the pathway.

One of the restaurants lining the Riverfront is Iron Hill Brewery, a chain of 12 area craft brew pubs, which we visit with some regularity (they have restaurants near where we live in New Jersey, and one close to my brother's home outside of Philadelphia). This is one of their original locations (named after the iron-smelting and shipment facility that was on the site).

On this delightful day, we asked to sit out on their patio deck overlooking the pathway and the river. Ray, our waiter, was a young, enthusiastic guy, and he was very knowledgeable about Iron Hill's range of seasonal and holiday beers. He asked what kind of beer we prefer. My wife and I told him that though we are only occasional beer drinkers, we like Blue Moon White IPA Belgian-style beer, and he suggested an Iron Hill Christmas-only beer (Santa's Little Helper), which tasted almost identical to Blue Moon, complete with coriander and orange peel in the recipe. Ray also recommended a predinner snack for my wife and me to nibble on as we watched the pedestrian traffic and small boats go by.

So far, so good. In fact, so far, so great. Ray was on a roll with us.

When he brought our beer and snack, Ray asked if we were regular Iron Hill patrons, and we replied that we enjoy the restaurant from time to time, but weren't what could be called frequent diners. In a nonpushy way, he then went on to explain about Iron Hill's "King of the Hill Rewards Club." He said that he thought it was a great deal, that it would quickly pay for itself and for the $25 annual fee we'd get:

- A $25 credit, based on points earned at purchase, after just a couple of visits
- A free handmade Iron Hill beer mug
- A free gift on our birthdays
- Invitation to exclusive club events throughout the year
- Directs e-mail contact with the head brewer about upcoming releases and events
- Any unused points rollover until next year

Sold!! We liked the way Ray, a committed ambassadorial server, presented the club rewards, as well as its simplicity and personalized benefits. And, he must have sensed that I love mugs (which was given to me, in a nice Iron Hill bag, during this visit—so, the bonus of instant gratification). Painlessly, Ray added the cost of membership to our bill for the beers and snack. The Delaware Valley is an active player in the growing brew pub movement. Iron Hill brewery gets my vote.

I'm always curious to learn what motivates employees to sign up patrons for their company's rewards program, so I asked Ray directly: "What do you get from Iron Hill when you bring in a new member?" When he replied "Nothing," I believed him. Ray went on to say that "I just like telling people about what we have, and to see our guests get good value and more frequently enjoy what Iron Hill has to offer." Ray is the kind of employee every company wants—an ambassador, focused on the company itself, the product/service value proposition, and the customer. Ray made my day.

Intersecting Viral Marketing with Emotional Customer Value Delivery Through Employee Ambassadorship: The TD Bank "Home Run"

As customers in all b2b and b2c sectors steadily become more actively digitized in their daily lives, companies are having to respond, and hopefully stay ahead, in the race to build stronger interpersonal relationships with them. Who's doing this well, using innovative techniques, actively leveraging employees, and setting standards for others to follow? For me, a great example is TD Bank, where viral communication meets real, and valued, experience delivery on a personalized, and deeply emotional, level.

Here's a quick thumbnail summary of where some examples of TD Bank's unique granular marketing and communication initiatives have taken the company over the past year or so.

—Early in 2015, in a campaign called "Make Today Matter," TD Bank gave 24 customers in 24 different cities—one a day for 24 days—24 hours to initiate projects that would benefit their local communities. Each individual was given approximately $30,000 to put toward launching the program. Customers were selected through a two-step process:

(a) an informal Facebook poll to generate ideas and (b) branch employees making the final selection based on their knowledge of customers.

TD created a microsite to collect and display "Make Today Matter" stories, and they posted local community program achievements, as varied as trail restoration to puppy adoption, in market locales such as Southern Florida and Philadelphia. The mini-documentary TD Bank created about the campaign has been viewed over five million times on YouTube.

—In July of 2015, TD Bank released a YouTube video, which got four million views in just five days. The video chronicled customer reactions to the deeply personal and emotional response to the unexpected gifts they received through a TD Bank promotion.

Earlier video campaigns like "TD Thanks You," where ATMs gave customers personalized gifts, and received over 20 million views, began this "out of the box" approach, absolutely unique in the retail banking world. It was one of the most successful marketing programs of 2014.

TD Bank has had a "Bank Human Again" communication theme for about the past two years with their customers (and potential customers), featuring relationship/transactional experiences and branch interactions, and with "store" employees, acting as bank ambassadors. This long-running campaign has distinguished TD Bank from its retail competitors. There is a strong recognition that while the company has to be as digitally efficient as its peers, there is an intersection where real conversations take place with real bank people, whether in customer support or at the local TD Bank branch. Also, the company leads by using assertive offline and online viral techniques to drive community awareness and new customer acquisition, perhaps the most innovative in the industry.

The "Bank Human Again" campaign has broadened and deepened its core messages, now communicated by TD Bank in an impressive array of media channels: movie screens, television, social media, Internet ads, outdoor, and mobile.

TD Bank stays ahead of its competition by leveraging employee ambassadorship. For example, they have learned that, overwhelmingly, customers prefer being thanked in person, as compared to telephone, e-mail, text, or other methods of contact. Results of their recent path-finding consumer study *The Art of Appreciation* (Figure 9.1) confirm this. Among key findings were that personal expressions of gratitude created

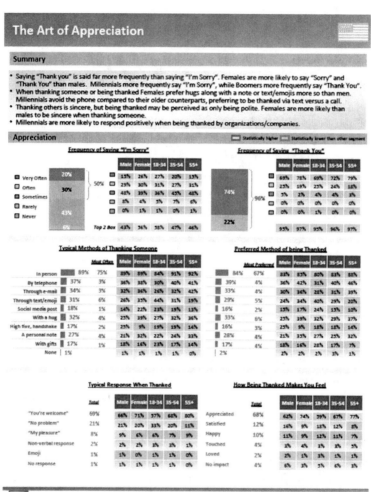

Figure 9.1 **TD Bank study** The Art of Appreciation

Source: TD Bank.

more positive feelings (77% positive to 23% neutral, with no negatives) among all key demographic groups:

- Male—75 percent positive, 25 percent neutral
- Female—80 percent positive, 20 percent neutral
- 18 to 34 years—81 percent positive, 19 percent neutral
- 35 to 54 years—76 percent positive, 24 percent neutral
- 55+ years—75 percent positive, 25 percent neutral

Further, the TD study has found that being thanked makes customers feel appreciated, deepening their relationship with, and trust in, the bank. Being thanked in person requires that customer-focused and customer-sensitive employees be hired. Especially where more complex banking interactions are concerned, this is particularly important. In a time when the number of bank branches in the United States continues to decline, brick and mortar locations sustain as key element in opening accounts, enhancing the customer's understanding of bank products, and reducing problems and complaints. Doing this well necessitates investment in locating, onboarding, and training staff to be committed employee ambassadors.

As a customer, and irrespective of business sector, there's nothing more brand-building, and image reinforcing, than feeling good about the human, personal, and emotional story a company you're affiliated with presents to its base and the public at large. For employees, there is great value in building job experiences that enable and deepen customer relationships. I'm a TD Bank customer and a strong, supportive advocate for the brand.

Holacracy: What Might Enhance Employee Experience and Productive Life Cycle … or Get in the Way

Tony Hsieh, the CEO of Zappos, has put a unique management and HR model into place. It's called holacracy, an approach to organizational redesign. This is a project he began in 2013. Holacracy, long story short, eliminates most formal titles and company supervisory levels, replacing them with self-organization and self-management Figure 9.2.

Holacracy, as a day-to-day enterprise operating approach, is also both controversial and uncomfortable for some. Even in a very progressive company like Zappos, this change has not gone down particularly well (Hsieh sent an e-mail to employees advising all Zappos staff that they had until the end of April 2015 to make a stay/go decision), as close to 20 percent of employees have left the organization. One CX research and consulting company believes that these departures will not hurt employee commitment, and by extension their role as ambassadors inside and

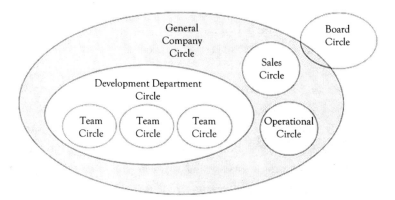

Figure 9.2 Holacratic organizational diagram

Source: Organization at the Leading Edge: Introducing Holacracy™ by Brian Robertson in *Integral Leadership Review* Volume VII, No. 3—June 2007.

outside of the company; but, that said, it's challenging to see how there's anything particularly positive for customers in this culturally modifying move.

The issue isn't so much that Tony Hsieh has made the decision to morph the company culture, architecture, and operational platform. It's that the effect, or potential effect, of this change on customers has not been thoroughly studied or discussed and has yet to unfold. Further, there's little evidence that this issue, that is, customer behavior impact, has been taken into consideration at all.

CEOs have certainly been known to make major unilateral moves like this, and there is probably something in their personalities that leads them to assume they can anticipate the marketplace reaction and enterprise cultural impact. Sometimes they're right, sometimes they're wrong.

In 2015, Howard Schultz, the now-retired founder and CEO of Starbucks, pushed forward with his "Race Together" concept. This was met with so much resistance, rather quietly from inside the company (as might have been expected) and more vocally and more negatively from customers, that the initiative was quickly withdrawn. Schultz claimed that the objectives he'd defined had been met, but that explanation felt more like backfill for an idea that was questionable at best and controversial and image threatening at worst.

In the case of Zappos, the "pay to quit" deal has long been offered to new employees if they feel they don't fit with the culture, or the culture isn't right for them. They receive one month's pay if they select this option. Normally, only about 1 to 3 percent of new hires make the choice to leave the employ of Zappos. At close to 15 percent, the "holacracy or resign," that is, my way or the highway, edict may have much more lasting and serious impact on the culture and on customers.

Many management scientists are skeptical about holacracy. Often, holacratic corporate systems have failed, and they have also been proven difficult to scale. Unilaterally moving his company to an arguably more utopian style of operations and employee interaction is an initiative some have felt is open to question. Observers feel that Tony Hsieh has put his highly successful enterprise at some risk, and maybe more than he'd like to believe. What is the real price, to employees and customers, of such a massive culture change?

A Quick Note: Employee Ambassadorship Versus Employee Advocacy

Similar to the how proponents of customer recommendation have endeavored to equate what is essentially an attitudinal macro measure with advocacy behavior, there has been a recent trend to conflate employee advocacy and employee recommendation of their employer with employee ambassadorship. A profound difference exists.

Employee advocacy, as some consulting organizations are defining it, is principally the ability of those inside the organization to communicate, largely through social means, a degree of credibility and transparency to the outside world. Here is how one consultant defined it:

> People want to know what is going on "behind closed doors" within certain companies and how they deal with successes and failures. ... When the public sees that the employees would personally recommend their company's service or product to their direct network, they surely have confidence in the quality and stand by the brand.

So, this particular "take" on ambassadorship is that employees have a role in creating social brand value. They are "brand ambassadors," individuals selected to communicate the social brand, specifically supporting the credibility of the company and its operations. One of the companies making this case is the Digital Influence Group, which has gone so far as to identify organizations with the highest combined levels of brand strength, brand popularity in social media, and social employees (Figure 9.3).

Their thesis is simple. If employees are happy, they will be more likely to put the brand in a positive light, both online and offline. The advice they offer for doing this is to create a brand ambassadorship unit within the company; but, first, a strong company culture is needed.

While having positive and vocal employees, who will trumpet the company's and brand's virtues both online and offline, is important, it is even more essential for the employees to be fully committed to the company, the value proposition, and, most especially, the customers through the delivery of value. It is the stakeholder-centric component of culture

Figure 9.3 Social employees

Source: Digital Influence Group.

and employee behavior that has morphed (or, more accurately, claimed to morph) employee engagement to employee ambassadorship. And, while it might be useful to have a "unit" of employees within the organization who have a more defined and active ambassadorial role, the real value of employee ambassadorship is that everyone working for the enterprise has these responsibilities in their everyday experience and actions.

Four Powerful Rules to Create Employee and Customer Word-of-Mouth Programs

We've just looked at how consulting companies have begun to conflate what they describe as "employee advocacy," including recommendation, with employee ambassadorship. As demonstrated throughout the book, ambassadorship is principally about high commitment; but, just as with customer advocacy, there does also need to be a strong and consistently vibrant informal vocal component.

And, if there are enterprise initiatives to build stronger relationships between employees and their peers, and between employees and other stakeholders, consideration must be given to how this is achieved, tactically and strategically. One key method is word-of-mouth programs. It has been found (by Engagement Labs and other consultants specializing in informal offline and online communication) that word of mouth is a solid, real metric that drives corporate revenue, so it is important that an effective stakeholder program be in place.

For any offline or online social word-of-mouth initiative to be impactful with key stakeholders, financially and otherwise, there must first be full realization of what it can and can't do, and what it is and what it isn't.

Based on broad employee and customer word-of-mouth program experience with b2b and b2c clients around the world, four general "rules" for accomplishing this can be put forward:

1. **Be authentic, transparent, and honest**. Saying that today's consumers and employees are "savvy" is only scratching the surface of their awareness, sophistication, and levels of discrimination in identifying what is real and what is fake. Informal communication programs can work, if and because both stakeholder groups feel they are

getting information and advice from individuals and entities they know and trust. Messaging and positioning statements provided by companies must be up-front and credible because, if they are not (or perceived as not), the backlash results of negative word of mouth can be significant.

2. **Be both strategic and tactical**. Use of online and offline social communication media isn't a replacement for advertising and other forms of stakeholder interchange, but it is an effective partner for succeeding with individual initiatives and long-term dialogue and inclusion. It must also be recognized that people and processes in a business model, representing "inside-out" advocacy creation with customers and ambassadorship with employees, are a priority before effective word-of-mouth initiatives can, or should, be launched. Much of the evidence of tactical and strategic success of informal communication programs has been because companies were passionate about stakeholders in the first place and made them feel like emotionally connected members of the family.

3. **Seek to leverage and influence, not control**. Up until electronic interaction—the Internet and wireless devices for accessing the Web on a mobile basis—changed the character of communication and engagement forever, companies frequently deluded themselves that they were in control of the awareness and influence processes. While multimedia, megabudget programs were extolling wonderful products and services (and social values) offered by corporations, product quality and service performance for customers, and evidence of a customer-centric culture for employees, was often in decline in the real world. Now, if experiences didn't at least match the brand and promises made through these communication programs, stakeholders express their feelings and opinions to the world with a single mouse click; and companies have to pay attention or suffer the lasting consequences of negative word of mouth.

4. **Emphasize people and core emotional values over "corporate" positioning**. As noted earlier, stakeholders can subconsciously and emotionally sense when companies are being honest and authentic, and when they're not. It's about hiring the most customer-sensitive, proactive staff, training them to be customer focused, and making customer processes as friendly as possible. In other words, customer

centricity must become a mantra, where optimum product value, provision of superior experiences at all touch points, offline and online word of mouth, and brand perception are critical elements of every decision. It is, finally, a recognition that word of mouth is what people (customers and employees) think and say about an organization, not what the organization believes and says about themselves.

To summarize, stakeholders now expect more from social media, and are using it more, and more effectively, than ever before. Organizations will need to move past the fear of change and experimentation, which social media represents to many C-suite executives.

The fear, it must be acknowledged, is not baseless. Most social communities are minimally monitored or controlled. Quantifiable measurement can be a challenge. While much of the online social interaction is positive, there is definitely a "dark side" too.

Stakeholders can, and do, readily express their frustration and negativity over poor experiences. Channels such as Twitter, YouTube, Yelp, and Facebook (and Ripoff Report and Complaints Board) are open forums for disaffected, even angry, groups with special interests. Many now know the story of Canadian musician Dave Carroll, whose music video "United Breaks Guitars" has been viewed millions of times on YouTube. Getting past the concerns associated with lack of direct control is the first stage of adoption, and companies, at minimum, should be actively monitoring the social communication environment to gauge the opportunities for application.

Once past the listening and monitoring stage, companies should move to more active interaction, brand favorability cultivation, and emotional bonding, getting beyond looking at social media as a traditional mass communication tool, and utilizing these channels as a set of approaches and opportunities to make messaging more meaningful.

One of the challenges here is coordinating the social media selected with other communication channels, including communication by employees. Flexibility, and maintaining an approach that responds to changing stakeholder dynamics, is key. For instance, a 2009 social media use study by *MarketingSherpa* found that, among customers, learning about special offers and sales was a prime motivator for consumers to connect with companies through social media. Another factor was consumer interest in learning about new products and services from companies they were engaged with, indicating a desire for deeper, more strategic, and personalized relationships.

Beyond the opportunity for direct interaction and relationship building, a related challenge is identifying methods for collecting data produced through offline and online interchange, and driving intelligent decision making and action. Studies indicate that many companies are now using social media in their communication efforts; however, most lack a consistent mechanism to measure the effect of their programs.

This is where an emotion-inclusive framework like advocacy measurement is a tremendous advancement in understanding customer behavior drivers and results, mirrored in ambassadorship measurement with employees. Whether obtaining stakeholder information online or offline, or communicating online or offline as a result of an experience, this type of research identifies the impact of perceived value on stakeholder actions. This is true, of course, in both b2b and b2c environments.

As concluded in a 2010 white paper by marketing software company Neolane:

With the right technology, skill sets, and C-level buy-in, social media provides an opportunity to take a more personalized and interactive approach to achieve true engagement. ... So, stop broadcasting, start engaging and put your social media intelligence to work.

Word of mouth has long been proven to be a significant component of, and contributor to, downstream stakeholder behavior. It is a direct outcome of the subconscious, emotional, and memory elements of experience; and, following "rules" such as I've outlined at the beginning of this section, it must be baked in to any communications initiative. For employees, and their contribution as ambassadors, it wouldn't be a bad idea to bake this into their job description as well.

Enterprise Employee Behavior Challenges Remain ... and a Life Cycle Prescriptive

For organizations to recognize, and leverage, the power of multilayered enterprise commitment through experience, the new realities of employee emotional needs and life cycle requirements need to be addressed as priorities. At the core of commitment and experience, a key factor is how aligned employees, irrespective of function, location, or level, are with customer thinking and behavior.

As we have stated, there are often significant, impactful perception–reality differences between stakeholder groups. The degree to which employees can mirror, or accurately reflect, the perceptions and realities of value expressed by customers says a great deal about the level of enterprise transparency and customer centricity. It also has much to do with employee experience. Naive companies have numerous employee–customer disconnects, and natural, or truly stakeholder-centric companies have relatively few.

Here's a straightforward prescriptive: To narrow or eliminate the employee–customer differences, mind the gap, first by recognizing that gaps always exist between inside design and outside delivery and response. When companies are innovative and inclusive with staff, all parties benefit. The company gets more effective employees. Employees like the participation and learning. Customers like the improved processes and interactions. Another key advantage of conducting employee "mirror" or "reflection" research, and one not to be overlooked, is that, in all likelihood, competitors don't have this kind of insight. They're hearing only from the external constituent group, the customers, but not from the equally important internal representatives and deliverers of value, company employees.

Anything that prevents an employee—any employee in the organization—or detracts from delivering an optimum customer experience must be proactively identified and rectified. So, it should also be noted that, somewhere between *Career Planning, Career Development*, and *Termination*, and just as with customers in their supplier relationship, **Employment Risk** can set in. And, again like customers, organizations need methods of mitigating or eliminating risk. It's part of creating and sustaining ambassadorial behavior, a state of higher purpose, fulfillment, and action among employees.

So, the key question: How does the enterprise not just reduce *Employment Risk*, but build purpose and fulfillment, especially where staff experience, focus, and motivation are concerned? About 15 years ago, my colleague, Jill Griffin and I identified nine best "people first" employee experience practices for our coauthored book, **Customer Winback**. Of these, having a culture of trust and empowerment, active training and cross-training (an element of recognition and reward), open vertical and horizontal communication, and proactive career pathing are perhaps most important. There's not a particular order in which these should be addressed—all are consequential.

How these practices mesh and produce desired employee and customer value was nicely summarized by Claudia Saran, a KPMG Principal. In Episode 4, "***Building a Business with Purpose***," from a recent (October, 2016) series of business strategy videos her company produced, entitled "The Entrée," she said:

> It's really trying to tap into something deeper and capture the hearts and minds of your people…It's pride, and you want that as a leader. That's going to breed productivity, morale, retention; and those people are going to be ambassadors for your brand.

Ideally, every organization can benefit from an authentic culture, along with a committed corps of employee ambassadors, individuals who will advocate for the brand/corporate entity, inside and outside of the company. We've witnessed high levels of cultural cohesion and consistent ambassadorial behavior in companies that are fiercely, and successfully, stakeholder-centric (like TD Bank). And, we have also seen employee ambivalence and negativism in organizations that are more top-down autocratic, are operations-, sales-, or product-obsessed, and are less focused on "people first" stakeholder experience and value delivery (like Bank of America).

The prescriptive: Simple, get all employees as close to customers as possible, every day. Make certain that customer value delivery is an achievable accountability in every job description. Build this into every employee's career path, and the employee, customer, and enterprise will be richer for it.

For Employees to Deliver CX Excellence Throughout Their Life Cycle, Ancient Greeks Had Words for It: *Chronos* and *Kairos*

First, a little dictionary diving is required. The word *chronos* may be familiar to some. In ancient Greek, it means "time" or "order," like chronology or sequence. *Kairos* is probably less well known. It means, essentially, doing something at the right instance, in other words, a moment of truth or when something of significance happens. Chronos is quantitative. Kairos is qualitative. Both are essential in CX, and particularly for the role of employees in delivering superior, differentiated value (or in undermining or destroying it).

Employees' actions, including expressing themselves face-to-face and through digital means, directly and indirectly impact much of what we understand about CX-based emotion and memory, leading to downstream behavior. For customer management and high-quality experience and value delivery to be optimized, one of the changes that companies will have to institute is to start focusing on people, all of the employees within the enterprise. This can't be done just when new hires are coming into the organization. It must be continuous, that is, throughout the employee life cycle.

As stated earlier, tremendous investments have been made on technological innovations—interactive voice response (IVR) systems, call routing, multimedia integration, and the like—yet investment in people, and processes to support them, has been stagnant, lagging behind other efforts. To deliver on the promise technology offers in customer relationships, organizations need to prioritize staff performance. People have to be trained in what to do and when to do it (chronos and kairos), provided with the tools and empowerment to deliver value, given feedback about how they're doing, and rewarded if they are doing well.

Creating a chronos and kairos culture within the organization that nurtures loyalty, commitment, advocacy, and productivity from the moment the new hire walks through the door and throughout the life cycle of the employee will go a long way to sustaining customer loyalty behavior. The good news is that employees, particularly those in customer service, seek trust and trustworthiness, and they desire to be active contributors to that effort.

Afterword

Eyes on the Stakeholder Experience Value Prize

Have We, Through More Effective Leaders, Finally Entered the Era of the Emotionally Driven, Vocal Employee Ambassador?

That's my belief. And, building on recently completed, groundbreaking employee ambassadorship behavior research which, supports our perspective, there is convincing proof that we are.

As stated multiple times in the book, employees are the critical common denominator in optimizing the customer experience (CX). Making the experience for customers positive and attractive at each point where the company interacts with them requires an in-depth understanding of both customer needs and how what the company currently does achieve that goal, particularly through the employees. That means that companies must understand, and leverage, the impact employees have on customer behavior. Further, and equally important, they must focus on optimizing the employee experience.

Supporters of employee satisfaction and engagement research and training techniques, with their focus on retention, productivity, and fit or alignment with business objectives, have made some broad, bold, and often unchallenged, assertions with respect to how these states impact customer behavior. Chief among these is that beyond skills, everyday performance, and even commitment to act in the best interest of their employers, employees have natural tendencies and abilities to deliver customer value, fueled by emotion and subconscious intuition.

Though on the surface this sounds plausible, and even rather convincing, a thorough examination of how employee satisfaction and engagement link to customer behavior will yield only a tenuous, assumptive, and anecdotal connection. In other words, there is much vocal punditry, and even whole books, on this subject, but little substantive proof.

Powerful new research has produced results, which allow companies to identify current levels of employee commitment and provide actionable direction on how to help them become more contributory and active brand ambassadors. Employee ambassadorship, as a core concept and research protocol, was designed to build and sustain stronger and more commitment-based and rewarding employee experiences and also improved CXs, driving the loyalty and advocacy behavior of both stakeholder groups, and, in turn, increasing sales and profits.

It is often stated (especially by corporate CEOs) that the greatest asset of a company is its employees. This emotionally based research has uncovered specifically how an organization can link, drive, and leverage employee attitudes and behavior to expand customer–brand bonding and bottom-line performance—and this is revolutionary! Employee ambassadorship research can be combined with existing customer and employee loyalty solutions to provide companies with comprehensive and actionable insights on the state of their employees' attitudes and action propensities and how those may be affecting customer behavior.

Employee ambassadorship identifies new categories and key drivers of employee subconscious emotional and rational commitment, while it also links with the emotional and rational aspects of customer commitment. At the poles, these employee-focused commitment categories include:

- **Ambassadors**, the employees who are most committed to a brand. Ambassadors represent employees who are strongly committed to the company's brand promise, the organization itself, and its customers. They also behave and communicate in a consistently positive manner toward the company, both inside and outside.
- **Saboteurs**, the employees who are the least committed to a brand. Saboteurs are active and frequently vocal detractors about the organization itself, its culture and policies, and its products and services. These individuals are negative advocates, communicating their low opinions and unfavorable perspectives both to peers inside the company and to customers and others outside the company.

In any group of employees, irrespective whether it's a service department, technical specialists, or a branch office, there will be differing levels of commitment to a brand and company, its value proposition, and its customers. If employees are negative to the point of undermining, and even sabotaging CX value, they will actively work against business goals. However, if employees are ambassadors, and whether they interact with customers directly, indirectly, or even not at all, they will better service and support your customers.

Our research process brings in several components, which build on, but differ markedly, from traditional, or standard, employee satisfaction and engagement techniques:

- For one difference, the attributes we examine actively include a significant proportion that is customer focus related.
- Next, we incorporate multiple overall "value indicators," which examine personal commitment to the organization, degree of positive and negative word of mouth on behalf of the company's products and services, and strength of belief in the value of these products and services to customers.
- We also develop an emotional profile, that is, how employees feel about the work they do for the company, and identify what employees desire most in their jobs.
- Finally, we evaluate each of the attributes based on (a) how employees rate them, that is, agree/disagree, (b) how much the employees want them, and (c) their prioritized value to the organization.

Combined, the ambassadorship concept, research protocol, and training applications can lead and enable any organization to be more stakeholder centric and dynamic. Often this journey begins with the recognition of its value by enterprise leaders.

The Power of Servant Leadership to Build and Sustain Stakeholder Value

During a recent series of stakeholder behavior instructional workshops conducted for our clients, one of the strongest areas of interest among workshop participants was how to gain senior management support and sponsorship for various customer-related and employee-related initiatives. For both inspiration and answers regarding the best and most effective approaches to apply, and to make certain that we are dealing in reality, that is, what works versus dealing in theories from a 30,000-foot level, we go back about 50 years, to trailblazing ideas of the two "Fathers of Servant Leadership," Max De Pree and Robert Greenleaf.

If you don't recognize their names, you should get to know them, because their ideas will have much to offer future stakeholder-centric cultures. De Pree and Greenleaf have long been considered the most original thinkers in the art, science, and pure knacks associated with the power of leaders to shape and direct an enterprise for the better.

One of De Pree's most memorable quotes, for example, is, "The first responsibility of a leader is to define reality. The last is to say 'thank you.' In between, the leader is a servant." That's almost Zen-like in its simplicity, accuracy, and application, and they have inspired such well-known CEOs as Jack Welch, Jan Carlzon (Scandinavian Airlines), Horst Schulze (Ritz-Carlton Hotels), and Herb Kelleher (Southwest Airlines) in their thinking and management styles. We can also see servant leadership in the ideas of Ken Blanchard, Steven Covey, Peter Senge, and M. Scott Peck.

For those unfamiliar with De Pree and Greenleaf, and the leadership concepts they represent, here are some brief facts. Greenleaf, who died in 1990, is generally acknowledged to be the founder of the modern servant leadership movement. He worked for AT&T for over 40 years, researching management, development, and education of employees. What he observed during that time was that the top-down, authoritarian leadership style prevalent in U.S. companies was not effective in providing value for stakeholders. He took early retirement in 1964 to establish the Greenleaf Center for Servant Leadership, which is still active today.

In 1970, Greenleaf identified 10 principles in his essay *The Servant As Leader*, all of which can apply directly to how leaders help generate a customer-centric culture and create lasting value for all stakeholders:

- Listening—being receptive and understanding stakeholder needs
- Empathy—accepting and recognizing stakeholders as people
- Healing—being a force for transformation and integration

- Awareness—helping create open and personal self-awareness
- Persuasion—building consensus rather than forcing decisions by coercing others
- Conceptualization—ability to both manage and look beyond the day to day
- Foresight—understand lessons learned, present realities, and view the future
- Stewardship—all stakeholders hold the enterprise in trust for the greater good
- Commitment to the growth of people—intrinsic value beyond basic contributions
- Building community—shaping and reinforcing relationships within the enterprise

If these 10 principles seem like they would be applicable to stakeholder centricity in operations and experiences, and humanistic approaches for building relationships and value within an enterprise, it's not an accident. Today, though many enterprise leaders still believe in, and practice, a paradigm that depends on controlled communication and power rather than mutually beneficial agreements, Greenleaf strongly believed otherwise. His "best test" for any enterprise effectiveness was to ask how leaders could serve people, help them grow as individuals, become more autonomous, healthier, wiser, and freer, and, themselves, become servants (see Figure A.1).

Figure A.1 Operating qualities of servant leaders

Source: Internet.

Certainly, we can see Greenleaf's legacy in organizations identifying themselves as agents of conscious capitalism. In a later essay *The Institution as Servant*, Greenleaf wrote:

> If a better society is to be built, one that is more just and more loving, one that provides greater opportunity for its people, then the most open course is to raise both the capacity to serve and the very performance as servant of existing major organizations by new regenerative forces operating within them.

That may feel squishy to some, but it should be recognized that such organizations have the capacity to become engines of growth and profitability, and many of these companies have done exactly that.

Max De Pree was the CEO of the Herman Miller office furniture company, his family's business, through the late 1980s. His 1987 book *Leadership Is An Art* has sold more than 800,000 copies, and this was followed up by *Leadership Jazz* in 1993. He established the De Pree Center for Leadership in 1996. Like Greenleaf, De Pree believes that leadership is not about telling others what to do, running their lives through pressure, and narrowly defining their world. It is about creating circumstances that allow individuals to assume responsibility and giving them the freedom to participate, collaborate, and work in the best possible way, fitting to who they are, and focusing on personal responsibility. This is engagement, building toward ambassadorship.

As De Pree has wisely stated:

> The signs of outstanding leadership appear primarily among the followers. Are the followers reaching their potential? Are they learning? Serving? Do they achieve the required results? Do they change with grace? Do they manage conflict? Leaders must understand who should be listened to and when. Leadership is liberating people to do what is required of them in the most effective and humane way possible. Leadership is much more an art, a belief, a condition of the heart, than a set of things to do. The visible signs of artful leadership are expressed, ultimately, in its practice.

The core precepts, and benefits of servant leadership, have been understood for centuries. In the *Tao Te Ching*, attributed to Lao-Tzu, it was written:

The highest type of ruler is one of whose existence the people are barely aware. Next comes one whom they love and praise. Next comes one whom they fear. Next comes one whom they despise and defy. When the servant leader's task is accomplished and things have been completed, all the people say "We ourselves have achieved it!"

Leaders of organizations desiring to be customer centric, and managers wanting to help leaders achieve that worthwhile goal, would do well to follow these ideals and the principles of Greenleaf and De Pree.

Where CX is concerned, it is important to remember that organizations and brands that want to succeed in today's competitive climate have successfully embedded CX into their cultures, from the C-level executive to the frontline employee. They prosper by using insights generated from a variety of channels and touch points, including employees, integrated with customer data from multiple sources, mined by sophisticated text analytics technologies, and then channeled to steer every corner of their businesses.

The more successful the brand, the more evident that the approaches taken in leadership are both bottom up and top down. This helps ensure a more strategic and real-world view of stakeholder behavior. Truly effective organizations have leaders committed to the stakeholder experience at every level and in every corner of the enterprise. These leaders focus on both individual and collective accomplishment.

This kind of achievement and fulfillment requires that experiences be optimized for all stakeholders. It's a simple, basic idea, but it works—now and for the future. Ideally, there should be a direct linkage back and forth between the leader, the employee, and the customer. This is where employee ambassadorship, like the edelweiss flower, can bloom and grow.

Index

CPSIA information can be obtained
at www.ICGtesting.com
Printed in the USA
FSOW02n0626250417
33424FS